The Ultimate Day Trader

HOW TO ACHIEVE CONSISTENT DAY TRADING PROFITS IN
STOCKS, FOREX, AND COMMODITIES

JACOB BERNSTEIN
Chief Market Analyst, Daily Sentiment Index

Avon, Massachusetts

Published by
Adams Business, an imprint of Adams Media, a division of F+W Media, Inc.
57 Littlefield Street, Avon, MA 02322. U.S.A.
www.adamsmedia.com

ISBN 10: 1-60550-008-9
ISBN 13: 978-1-60550-008-9

Printed in the United States of America.

10 9 8 7 6

Library of Congress Cataloging-in-Publication Data
is available from the publisher.

This publication is designed to provide accurate and authoritative information with regard to the subject matter covered. It is sold with the understanding that the publisher is not engaged in rendering legal, accounting, or other
professional advice. If legal advice or other expert assistance is required, the
services of a competent professional person should be sought.
—From a *Declaration of Principles* jointly adopted by a Committee of the
American Bar Association and a Committee of Publishers and Associations

Many of the designations used by manufacturers and sellers to distinguish
their product are claimed as trademarks. Where those designations appear
in this book and Adams Media was aware of a trademark claim, the designations have been printed with initial capital letters.

This book is available at quantity discounts for bulk purchases.
For information, please call 1-800-289-0963.

Dedication

This book is dedicated to the thousands of traders all over the world who have been loyal followers of my work. Your suggestions have helped me learn and grow. Although we are all players in the most difficult trading game in existence, we have also helped each other grow by example, by learning, and by persistence.

—Jake Bernstein
Santa Cruz, CA
March 2009

Acknowledgments

I thank the following individuals and/or organizations for their assistance in various forms:

To Peter Archer of Adams Media who had his patience tested to the limit with my tardiness. To my family who was also patient in the time I took from them to write this book. To the good people at Genesis Financial Technologies for permission to use their charts and software. To my office staff for their never-ending patience and help. To my literary agent Michael Steinberg who, in spite of me, remains my agent, and to the many traders out there who have used, believe in, and supported my work

—Jake Bernstein

Contents

Introduction 1

| Part I | The General Principles of Day Trading | 15 |

Chapter 1 Definitions and Directions—What It Means
to Day Trade Today 17

Chapter 2 The Need for Methods 27

Chapter 3 An Overview of Day Trading Markets and
Methods 53

Chapter 4 The Importance of Structure and the STF
Framework 73

| Part II | Successful Methods of Day Trading | 83 |

Chapter 5 Gap Day Trading 85

Chapter 6 The Moving Average Channel with Confirmation
Trend and Channel Trading 109

Chapter 7 Day Trading By the Day 125

Chapter 8 Volume Spikes and Their Use in Day Trading 139

Chapter 9 Day Trading With Divergences: Set-Up 151

Chapter 10 Day Trading with Divergence: Momentum
Timing Triggers 177

Chapter 11 Day Trading With Divergence: Follow-Through 193

Chapter 12 The Stochastic "POP" Method 205

Chapter 13 The Trend Breakout Method 221

Part III	At the End of the Day	243

Chapter **14** Trading in a News-Driven Market 245
Chapter **15** Exit Strategies 259
Chapter **16** The Pragmatics of Day Trading 275
Chapter **17** Putting It All Together 291
Chapter **18** Ten Cardinal Rules of Day Trading 303
Conclusion 318
Glossary 325
Resources 337
Index 339
About the Author 345

Introduction

Change creates opportunity. While investors and traders often fear the consequences of change, for day traders change in market trends creates opportunities for profit. At no time in the history of the stock and commodity markets have such opportunities been as promising or as plentiful as they are today. Why? Because never before have changes in market trends been as swift, as frequent or as large as they are today.

While the importance of long-term market trends over one year or more cannot be denied, the numerous short-term and intra-day opportunities in today's markets offer heretofore unheard of profit potential to day traders. In the case of crude oil futures, for example, the price range in one day can go as high as $6,000 per contract. The typical price range for crude oil futures in 1998 went from about $800 to $1,600 in one day. Clearly, the change has been dramatic.

The factors that have combined to nourish this seemingly "best of all possible day trading worlds" are several and substantially varied. They include the rapid growth of electronic order entry, fully computerized trading, the influx of substantial risk capital through hedge funds and sovereign wealth funds (adding liquidity to the markets), significant advances in Internet speed connectivity, the development of advanced trading and charting software, as well as the persistent decline in commission costs. Traders can trade faster and cheaper than ever before.

But can they trade better? Have the tools and techniques for day trading improved commensurate with profit-making opportunities? Has the lot of the typical day trader improved

1

or stagnated? Has the advent of twenty-four-hour trading provided new opportunities for profits or pitfalls for losses? Has the foreign currency (FOREX) market truly been a new source for profits or simply a new vehicle for professional trader and broker/dealer profits?

Yes, change creates opportunity. But does opportunity create profits? No! Opportunity opens the door to potential profits but we must still walk through that door safely, sanely and with clear direction. *The Ultimate Day Trader* will show you that door and give directions on how to walk through it. After all, you're the one who's doing the walking.

NEW ERA—OLD ISSUES

We have entered a new era of trading and investing that, although promising, is fraught with risk. Instead of a two-sided coin on which one side is "change" and the other side "opportunity," we need to think of a multifaceted polyhedron that reads "change," "opportunity," "risk." I emphasize this because many traders and investors, blinded by the lure of profits and inspired by the promise of technology, have either ignored or underplayed the risk side of the equation. In and of itself such myopic behavior is not unusual. In today's markets, more than ever, to ignore risk is an invitation to disaster. Truth be known, I believe that many brokerage houses and trading platform providers have, in their fervor to promote day trading, significantly under-represented the risks.

To ignore risk and focus only on potential reward is hardly unique in market history. During the Dutch Tulip Mania of the 1600s, speculators bought and sold tulip bulbs of minimal intrinsic value. Nonetheless speculators paid the equivalent of thousands of dollars for a single bulb. Without a doubt they were focused on the opportunity while underplaying the concomitant risks and realities. In their never-ending pursuit of profits, many market players have embraced day trading as their vehicle to riches. Much to the chagrin of many, their dreams rarely become realities. The reasons for their failure are clear and unmistakable. Let's examine two of the most prominent reasons:

1. There is the simple and undeniable fact that *most day traders are nothing more than amateur gamblers.* They bring to the business of day trading an orientation that is not consistent with the necessary principles of solid risk management and profit maximizing strategies.
2. Most aspiring day traders lack a consistent and logical trading methodology, a functional knowledge of order placement, sufficient funds, and self-discipline, as well as the hands-on experience essential to succeed in the most demanding of all financial games.

Given this sad but true situation, the aspiring trader must overcome numerous obstacles to achieve consistent profitability. While this book will provide you with a number of technical tools that I believe will assist you in your quest for profits, I will also attempt to address issues that may impede your progress. Recognizing the fact that even the best tools can be rendered less than effective by limiting factors such as the two reasons stated above, I will offer you some cogent solutions and directions that will facilitate your success if you apply my methods properly and consistently.

PROMISES, PROMISES

Day trading has always been a favorite arena for purveyors of hype and hope. In late 2007, an Internet search of the phrase "profitable trading" returned 376,000 results. Among the lines:

- "Learn successful trading"
- "How to Develop a Profitable Trading System"
- "Profitable Trading System Secrets"
- "Options Made Easy: Your Guide to Profitable Trading"
- "Profitable Trading Techniques"
- "135% '07 Return so Far"
- "Day Trading 90% Accurate"
- "Big Profits Up and Down"

The list drones on with the same theme for literally hundreds of pages.

An Internet search of the phrase "day trading" returns 8.1 million results! The promises, guarantees, profit potential, and claims range from the utterly absurd to the downright impossible. Sadly, there are far too many gullible investors who, enticed by the pandering pitch, are ready to part with their hard-earned money to learn the art and science of day trading. Lured by the prospect of making a living from the financial markets, they have become victims of what I call the "Great Day-Trading Robbery."

But let's not throw the baby out with the bath water. It's not all bad. Somewhere within the haystack of outrageous claims are a few precious needles of truth. It is my goal to share some of these with you within the pages of this book. What I am about to share has been acquired through hands-on trading experience over the last forty years, combined with extensive research on trading methods and systems.

My goal is not only to teach you the methods that I have discovered through trial and error as well as through research but also to warn you about the possible psychological and behavioral pitfalls of each approach. To simply present a manual of systems and methods would not address one of the major issues that impede trader success—and that issue is trader psychology (or perhaps more appropriately named "trader behavior").

NO SHORTAGE OF SELF-HELP TOOLS

Since the 1970s a plethora of books, investing magazines, newspapers, seminars, video courses, online courses, newsletters, and infomercials, as well as radio and television business reports have bombarded the investing public with advice, techniques, systems, methods, tools, trading programs, and get-rich-quick schemes.

In addition, the major financial exchanges, in a quest to build trading volume and visibility and to compete with each other, have sold the public on the promise of short-term trading and day trading, making access to the markets easier than ever. While real estate was once the chosen vehicle by which the American financial dream could be fulfilled, that game has become difficult, given the downturn in the market. Trading has had its ups and downs too, with a big boom brought on in part by new and widely available Internet tools in the late 1990s, followed by a bust with the dot-com crash shortly thereafter.

That bust served to weed out the weak hands, but the practice still flourishes. And for some, day trading has been the new real estate as that boom fades into oblivion. But the popularity of day trading has also created numerous challenges.

Recognizing the challenges that confront the day trader—and recognizing the profit opportunities from repeated electronic trades for brokers and platform providers—many (perhaps too many) tools have been developed to assist the aspiring day trader. Naturally, these tools will cost you, as a trader, money. But price in and of itself is no measure of efficacy. I have found that some of the simplest methods that are available at no cost can be just as effective as those with absurdly high price tags. Less can often be more. I'll talk more about this later in the book.

TOO MANY CHOICES CREATE CONFUSION

Adding to the day-trading landscape is a vast and ever-increasing number of financial instruments available to investors and traders since the dawn of the twenty-first century. Complexity and diversity reign supreme. Among the choices from which investors can select their means to an end are:

- Stocks
- Futures
- Options on stocks
- Options on futures
- Interest-rate–related vehicles
- Long Term Equity Anticipation options on stocks (LEAPS)

- Exchange traded funds (ETFs)
- Single stock futures
- Cross currency spreads
- Spread betting (in England)
- Australian Contracts For Difference (CFDs)
- The FOREX (short for Foreign Exchange Market, trading in cash currency)

In addition, there are variations on the theme of ETFs, (i.e., "double short" or "double long" as well as "triple short" and "triple long"). The list grows daily. It's enough to confuse even the most experienced trader or investor, let alone the tyro.

THE DAY TRADING CHALLENGE

The task that awaits those who seek to play the financial game on their own is formidable but not insurmountable. Aspiring day traders as well as those with some experience in the field must become educated in methodology but also choose a vehicle or vehicles that will hopefully take them to their goal with a minimum of risk and capital outlay with relative ease and rapidity. Regardless of choice, the newcomer faces fierce and growing competition from those who have already learned to play the game successfully and, of course, from professionals whose goal it is to separate the inexperienced from their funds.

Have I scared you off? I hope not. Yes, trading is a difficult game. The journey to success is arduous. The path is fraught with risk. But the good news is that the game can be won. A pot of gold awaits those who learn their lessons well and who

7

persist. The bad news is that many will either quit the game or lose their speculative funds before they can achieve even a moderate degree of success.

Those who seek to convince you that the trading game (whether day trading or short-term trading) is simple, attainable by everyone, or easily learned are misleading you. Trading is no less a business than operating a retail store or being a physician. There are solid, time-tested, clear, and teachable principles underlying success. Not everyone can be a physician. Nor can everyone be successful at running a retail business. The same holds true for day trading. In my view, underlying intelligence, family background, social class, or education are not nearly as important to success in trading as are persistence, the motivation to succeed, self-confidence, self-discipline, sufficient starting capital, organization, and emotional stability. Of these, the weakest links in the chain are starting capital and the emotional correlates that are part and parcel of the trading process.

WHY THIS BOOK?

I should start right off by warning you that this book is not designed for the first-time day trader. My purpose in *The Ultimate Day Trader* is to introduce not just specific trading methodologies and techniques but also a guiding philosophy and thought process for how to use them. From that base I also discuss more generalized philosophy and pragmatics about being a trader, from start to finish of the trading day, week and month; in short, your life as a day trader. While these concepts certainly apply to the novice trader, they will be much easier to grasp for someone who has had some day trading experience. A true beginner at day trading might be better served to pick up a copy of *A Beginner's Guide to Day Trading Online* by Toni Turner (2nd ed., Adams Media, 2007).

As I enter my fourth decade in the markets as a trader, analyst, author, educator, and trading system developer, I find that while some aspects of trading have grown by leaps and bounds other areas have barely advanced. Indeed, the weakest link in the chain remains the trader. It is a sad but true fact of market life that even the most profitable trading systems and methods will, in the hands of an undisciplined trader, be rendered worthless or even dangerous. I liken the situation to that of a high-powered, high performance-racing vehicle being piloted by an inexperienced driver. The results can be, and most often are, catastrophic. In preparing to write this book, I have asked myself some questions:

- What can be done to improve the lot of the average trader?
- Are the solutions to this dilemma to be found in more education, psychiatry, faster computers, better software, better systems, or a combination of the above?
- Do better systems create better traders?
- Is the ability to trade profitably innate or can it be learned?
- Is day trading the best way to succeed in the markets, or is investing the true key to consistent profits?

I have made my best attempt to answer these and other essential questions in this book. Beyond that, I have other reasons for putting this book together:

- To provide an overview of the day trading spectrum within the context of changes that have taken place since 1997 when I authored *The Compleat Day Trader* (McGraw-Hill, 1997).
- To introduce new day trading methods that are applicable to today's more volatile and dynamic markets
- To teach order entry strategies designed to vastly improve the odds of success
- To show you how to prevent careless but costly errors when using electronic trading platforms
- To present, discuss, and provide a detailed profit maximizing strategy for each of the strategies I have developed
- To illustrate all strategies clearly, visually, and with detailed examples
- To disclose all of the risks that are inherent in day trading
- To explore potentially new avenues and methods of day trading

I will do all these things, providing detailed illustrations, rules, and a summary of the good and bad points associated with each method I explain. While I cannot guarantee these methods will work as well in the future as they have in the past, I do believe that, at the very minimum, they will provide you with solid rules, objective methodologies, and directions for integration with the work you may currently be doing in the markets.

A SHORT LIST OF PERSONAL GOALS

I have some additional goals not directly related to those stated above. Rather, they are more personal than market related and come from years of experience and impressions of the practice of day trading:

Give back. I have a sincere and unending desire to bring traders good information in order for them to be successful. I do this because the markets have, in many ways, been very good to me and I believe that we must all give something back to society. I'm no Warren Buffett, but I do share many of his beliefs about giving back.

Get the story right. Through the years unethical, unscrupulous, and unsavory characters have literally stolen many of my original ideas and methods in the stock and commodity business. These individuals have no respect for what has been developed through the hard work and financial expense of others. Sadly, they often pervert, subvert, or simply explain my methods incorrectly. Because the methods in this book are essentially or entirely my methods, they should be presented correctly. In a very few cases my work is derived from the published ideas of others. In such cases I will provide appropriate credit. Hopefully, this book will go a long way in the direction of clarification and elucidation.

Level the playing field. Finally, I believe that professionals have always had the "edge" in the game of day trading. It's time to level the playing field in favor of the independent and/or smaller trader. It's a sad but true fact that professionals are not only privy to inside information, but they also exert a good deal of control over the markets, often running markets in the direction they desire. In the process, the average day trader stands little chance of success. On occasion the actions of insiders are either illegal or they border on the fringe of illegality. But given the financial and political power of these insiders and large traders, they are able to escape unscathed. I believe that my methods can help you minimize or possibly overcome the advantage that these individuals and/or institutions have over the average trader.

WHAT'S AHEAD?

The rest of this book is my best attempt to accomplish the following seven goals, with many more features and explanations along the way:

1. Give you an overview of the issues and obstacles that must be overcome in order to be consistently profitable as a day trader in stocks and/or futures
2. Provide you with objective, concise, and reliable trading methodologies to help you achieve trading profits in the single day time frame
3. Provide you with the necessary trading structure or model to facilitate the application of trading tools
4. Give you the rules necessary to minimize risk and to maximize profits
5. Show you how to select the best market candidates for day trading

6. Discuss the dos and don'ts of electronic order entry
7. Show you how to diversify your day trading portfolio to minimize periods of drawdown and improve stability of performance

A CHANGING MARKETPLACE

As I apply the finishing touches to this book, financial markets all over the world are in turmoil. Volatility reigns supreme. As a matter of fact, I have never, in my forty years of experience, seen any period of time that has been marked by such significant intra-day price swings. I am confident that the issues that have led to this situation will be resolved in a positive fashion. In the interim, however, the large intra-day price swings in virtually all markets will continue to provide numerous day trading opportunities and risks. I will state once again that *risk control and management of losses are the two most important aspects of trading.* If you fail to control risk then you will lose your speculative capital. As regards to loss management, without your speculative capital you are out of the game. You can't win the game if you can't play the game. It's obvious. It's simple, but it's essential.

I wish you the best of trading and I invite you to write me, if you have questions or if I can be of assistance.

My e-mail address: *jake@trade-futures.com*

—Jake Bernstein
Bonny Doon—Santa Cruz, California
March 2009

PART I

THE GENERAL
PRINCIPLES OF
DAY TRADING

Chapter **1**

Definitions and Directions—What It Means to Day Trade Today

Although, as I indicated in the introduction, this book is largely for the experienced trader, there may be some who are considering entering the market for the first time or who simply want to know more about day trading, preparatory to launching themselves into the market. For these readers, I present the following basic information.

What is a day trader? What, exactly does a day trader do? Simply stated, a day trader is an individual who enters and exits a position in the markets during the course of the trading day. For the purpose of this book we will consider a day trade to be a trade that is entered and closed out within the course of the day. It's a simple but clear definition. If, for example, you decide to keep a trade overnight, then it is really not a day trade and it does not conform to the rules I will present herein.

Has the definition of "day trade" changed now that twenty-four-hour trading is a reality in virtually all markets? A little further clarification is in order given the expanding landscape of trading hours in various markets.

REDEFINING THE "DAY TRADE"

As just mentioned, a day trade is a trade position entered and exited within a trading day. The number of hours in that day isn't so important; what is important is the *concept* of entering and exiting the market without taking a position home overnight.

The advent of twenty-four-hour trading in many markets has obscured the definition of the "day trade." As an example, consider the currency futures. The closing time for currency futures traded at the IMM exchange (Chicago) is 4:00 P.M. Central Time. The opening time for the "next day" is one hour later at 5:00 P.M. Hence, the market trades for twenty-three hours. Should we therefore define the trading day at twenty-three hours? Given the trading hours we have no choice but to do so. Slowly but ever so surely all of the futures markets are becoming electronically traded and they are open for as long as twenty-three hours. In the FOREX markets (cash currency trading) the market day is essentially twenty-four hours. In the U.S. stock market the trading day begins at 8:30 A.M. Central Time and ends at 3:00 P.M. Central Time. Nonetheless stocks can be traded in the "after market." As you can see, the traditional definition of the "day trade" is no longer applicable. What to do? Given current and developing conditions, here are my guidelines for length of a day trade:

Stock Markets: Trades executed during the day session in stocks are considered day trades. In the New York markets, for example, the trading hours are currently 9:30 A.M. Eastern Time through 4:00 P.M. Eastern time. Many stocks can be traded in the extended hours, but I will not consider extended hours trading as part of the definition for day trading in stocks.

Futures: Many futures markets currently have day sessions and extended sessions. As noted above, currency futures have a twenty-three-hour "day." In such cases I consider the entire twenty-three-hour day as fair game for a "day trade."

FOREX: The FOREX market is a cash currency market that trades round the clock. In this case, as in the case of currency futures cited above, I consider the entire twenty-four-hour trading day to be fair game for a day trade.

WHY DAY TRADE?

Now that we're clear on the definition of what a day trade is, let's ask a more complicated and strategic question: Why do it? Why limit yourself to getting in and out of the markets within a single trading day? Day traders offer a number of reasons in support of the single-day-trading approach. Here are some of them:

More effective use of margin, (funds borrowed from your broker). Many brokers charge less interest or none at all on money borrowed to buy securities if you close out the position before the end of the day.

Reduced headline risk. Day trading eliminates concerns about how overnight news might affect a position since you are out at the end of the trading day.

Lower margins. Day trade margins are often lower than holding a trade overnight.

Knowing the results. You know the "score" (i.e., your results) by the end of the day.

Market volatility. You can make plenty of money off of price swings within the trading day, and many of these swings have predictable patterns. Market volatility creates many opportunities during the single day time frame.

Low trading costs. Low commissions allow you to profit on relatively small price moves.

Instant execution. Virtually instant electronic price execution increases the odds of a good price execution and thereby extends the opportunity for profits.

Reliable forecasting. There are a number of predictable price patterns within the day time frame.

Diverse markets. There are a number of markets that lend themselves to day trading by virtue of their trading activity and volatility, and therefore you can trade a diversi-fied number of markets in the day time frame.

The process is enjoyable. For some, it's the thrill of the chase; it's like the excitement of betting on a horse and watching it win.

The challenge is appealing. Trading is intellectually chal-lenging and competitive, factors that appeal to many per-sonality types.

PASSION . . . AND HARD WORK

If you're an experienced trader, you may have additional thoughts or items to add to this list, things that you've found personally motivating in your career as a trader. However, I sug-gest that the rational reasons for day trading are not nearly as important as having a passion for it. Without a doubt the rea-sons offered above are a matter of opinion. Day trading is, at best, one of the most difficult undertakings in the world of trad-ing. Frequently traders will need to expend ten units of effort in order to achieve one unit of return. Are you satisfied with this equation or would you rather expend one unit of effort in order to achieve ten units of return by short-term (several days) or intermediate-term trading (several weeks or months). Can you do both? Yes, because they are not mutually exclusive.

The problem is that day traders often develop a particular mindset toward trading the stock, futures contract, or option that is the antithesis of the mindset needed for longer-term trading of an underlying company or a commodity. You'll take no interest in a company's products or in the underly-ing long-term fundamentals of growing corn. You're simply dealing in a security, buying it low and selling it high (or vice versa if going short), buying it higher and selling it higher, selling it short low and buying it back higher, trying to make a profit, trying to be a little smarter and a little faster than other players.

The mindset of the day trader is markedly different than the mindset of the investor or the short term trader. By definition a day trade must be closed out by the end of the "day." While the definition of the term "end of day" varies from market to market, the idea is the same. Trades must not be carried through to the next trading session. As such, the focus of the day trader is narrow. The goal of taking a profit is always in sight. The goal of limiting losses and/or placing stop losses at break even (i.e., the price at which a trade was entered) is always foremost in the day trader's mind. As the day progresses, the goal of taking a profit or eliminating risk becomes more important. The pressures of time and price are much more evident in the behavior of the day trader than they are in the behavior of the short-term trader or the investor. We can compare the day-trader mind set to that of the sprinter as opposed to that of the long-distance runner. The goal of the sprinter is to go as fast as possible and as safely as possible and to win. The long-distance runner has to pace his or her speed in order to finish the race.

Some people have trouble taking such a dispassionate or perhaps even mercenary view of what they buy and sell, and it may mean that trading isn't for them. As you read on, I hope you will get more comfortable immersed in a "total trading" role. How can this contradiction of terms be resolved? I will offer you some suggestions in the chapters that follow.

THE GOOD, THE BAD, AND THE UGLY SIDES OF TRADING

While the financial appeal of day trading is a powerful magnet, I'm sure that if you're familiar with it at all, you'll be aware that this promising venture also has a dark side. If you're nervous or unsure about your future prospects as a trader, I can offer you several reasons to avoid day trading. You should consider the following as well before you make the decision to day trade or to continue day trading:

- **It's hard, hard work.** The amount of effort required to day trade is often not commensurate with the return.
- **Random events are common.** Many of the price movements that occur during the course of the day are unpredictable and, therefore, day trading is often a low-accuracy venture. Those of you who like to work eight hours and earn a known sum of money for doing so, look out. Day trading probably isn't for you. The methods detailed in this book are intended to help tilt the odds in your favor by reducing your response to random events. This is achieved by using patterns that are predictable with a trade management approach that has been designed to maximize profits while reducing losses.
- **It'll suck up your bandwidth.** Day trading requires attention—depending on which method(s) you use you may need to be a "slave" to the market during the trading day, and some nightly and before-opening homework is suggested, too. At least two of the methods detailed in this book do not require moment by moment supervision.

- **It's competitive.** Day trading is highly competitive—You're in a challenging marketplace; for every winner there's a loser and everyone knows that. You're competing with professionals who often have better methods as well as inside information. Therefore your odds of success may be poor.

- **It's stressful.** We're talking real money here, and things may not happen as you'd expect them to. Day trading can often be very stressful. If you're easily frustrated, or prone to assume that the market, not you, is wrong, trading might be difficult for you. The key to overcoming the stress and the lack of discipline that can be caused by stress is to use a structured, consistent, step-by-step process as opposed to the "seat of the pants" or "guts trading" that typifies the behavior of most day traders.

In the end, only you can decide if you have the right mindset and tolerance range for risk and stress—as well as the financial ability—to successfully day trade. If you evaluate your characteristics and conclude day trading is not for you, that's fine. There are lots of other forms of investing or even short-term trading to get involved in. The important thing is to figure out what's right for you—what accomplishes your financial objectives while still being consistent with your personality and lifestyle—that's the one that's right for you.

Now that we have examined the case both for and against day trading, let's begin our detailed examination of the most risky and most rewarding game in town.

DAY TRADING IN THE PUBLIC EYE

Much has been made of whether or not day trading serves a useful purpose for markets and for society in general, or whether it is just a band of greedy gamblers looking to steal profits from well-intentioned investors. Editorial comments on the topic are all over the place.

Yes, it is true, traders are aggressively looking to profit from the markets and from other investors. They don't add much value in terms of providing capital for the function of free capitalist society or the companies and businesses within it. They are simply dealers in the market, like an antiques dealer or car dealer or a chicken seller at a bazaar. As such they provide a useful function by making a market, by buying here and selling there, by creating liquidity, that is, buying and selling choices, in the market. As they provide liquidity and counter-parties to other buyers and sellers, they help define the best price for the product and to make it transparent—that is, easy to see—to the public.

The presence of a large number of traders will reduce the "spread," that is, the difference between the bid, or buy, price and the ask, or sell, price to a minimum. Contrast this to a situation where there was only one dealer in a market—that dealer could make the spread almost anything he wanted and move the price at his own free will. The presence of traders makes the markets move more in line with true supply and demand and makes the price fair and transparent to everyone. So, while every vocation has its rogues, the profession of securities trading serves a useful purpose in moving the markets of capitalism forward.

DO WE HAVE WHAT WE NEED?

Yes, time and research have given us proven tools for success in the markets. The fact that we have tools in no way ensures that we can or will use them successfully. Nor does the fact that we have tools ensure that we have the skills to use them *effectively*. At times the rapidity of progress outpaces the experience required to translate progress into results. As an extreme example consider the development of atomic theory, first as the horrific atomic bomb and many years later as the immense promise of nuclear energy. Consider the development of the Internet, first as a means of military communication, then as tool for mass public communication via e-mail and instant messaging and finally as the most powerful tool ever developed for mass advertising and retail sales.

There is no doubt that every advance in technology has a positive as well as a negative side. The same vehicle that facilitates progress also opens the door to a host of negatives. Whether these downsides take the form of nuclear bombs, Internet scams, hacking, the dissemination of misinformation, disinformation, or much worse, we can either profit from or become victims of new technologies. I believe that we have the tools for success as day traders. I believe that they are effective, consistent, and easily applied. I believe that with a well-planned and implemented trading structure we can achieve success in the most difficult game around.

Chapter **2**

The Need for Methods

Day trading, which was once the exclusive domain

of the professional trader, has become the most

popular vehicle for today's aspiring speculators. Day

trading has become the favorite target of system

developers, advisory services, FOREX brokers, and

seminar promoters. The development of high-speed

computers, electronic trading, and the virtually

immediate dissemination of price quotes and news

have combined to enhance both the appeal of day

trading as well as the anticipated profit potential.

Add to the mix low commission costs, a backdrop of highly volatile economic and political news that create large intra-day price swings, and the participation of hedge funds and sovereign wealth funds as major market participants, and you have the primary reasons for the growing appeal of day trading.

Unfortunately that which attracts does not always fulfill its promise. While day trading does indeed offer significant profit potential, it is also the most volatile, most arduous, as well as the fastest game in town. Those who choose to enter the rarefied air of the day trading arena also choose to enter a venture in which consistent profits are difficult to achieve without an arsenal of clearly defined and objective tools. My emphasis is on the term "consistent." While many traders can score small or even large victories from time to time, the quintessential issue is whether they can consistently generate profits commensurate with their efforts. This is, of course, the underlying issue of all trading whether day trade, short-term, or long-term. *Consistency and constancy trump the gains achieved in small skirmishes.* Most day traders can win minor battles, however, in the end they lose the war—but why? Why is it so hard for traders to achieve *sustained* success? There is no single answer but there are many contributing factors to the "why" question. Among the top reasons for this sad but true state of affairs are:

- Lack of an effective trading methodology
- Insufficient trading capital
- Lack of discipline
- Inconsistent implementation of trading rules
- Lack of an objective trading plan
- Inability to maximize profits
- Over-trading

Without a doubt the challenge of profitable day trading is to overcome these significant obstacles. Can it be done? Are there time-tested strategies and methods that, combined with discipline, can help us win the day trading "war"? I say, "Yes."

While some would have us believe that our methods of day trading must adapt to changing market conditions, I believe that we already have the methods. What we need is to apply them correctly. As an example, trading methodologies that were profitable for day trading S&P 500 futures in the 1990s may very well not prove profitable today unless they use stop losses—downside protection setup to close out a position automatically if a certain loss criterion is met—that are large enough to allow for the wide daily price swings that have characterized the markets of 2007 and 2008. A stop loss of $1,500 below the trade price may have been sufficient then, but now that stop loss might be $3,500 or more.

Here is a clear illustration of my point. Consider the following performance histories of a short-term trading method that I developed for S&P 500 futures. The method that generated each performance history is the same. The only difference is the amount of the stop loss. By selecting the appropriate stop loss for the given market we can change a losing system into a winning system. While this may not be earth-shattering news to the experienced trader, the novice who has not been educated in such basics will find the facts quite revealing. Inasmuch as the typical day trader comes to the markets without sufficient education, the consequences of not knowing such information can be (and usually are) dire.

The following two sample reports illustrate the difference between the two stop loss settings, the first at $500, the second at $3,500. These summary reports, from the charting and analysis program I use, known as Genesis Navigator™, show the comparative results. Don't worry at this point about all the other facts and figures on these reports; some are more important than others and you'll learn about all of them eventually. These examples serve not only to point out the difference between the settings but to also give you a glimpse at a daily trading performance report.

SUMMARY

Overall			
Total Net Profit:	$63,630	Profit Factor ($Wins/$Losses):	1.44
Total Trades:	341	Winning Percentage:	19.9%
Average Trade:	$187	Payout Ratio (Avg Win/Loss):	5.77
Avg # of Bars in Trade:	0.23	Z-Score (W/L Predictability):	0.3
Avg # of Trades Per Year:	31.2	Percent in the Market:	2.5%
Max Closed-out Drawdown:	-$29,335	Max Intra-day Drawdown:	$-29,555
Account Size Required:	$46,873	Return Pct:	135.7%
Open Equity:	$0	Kelly Ratio:	0.0607
Current Streak:	1 Losses	Optimal f:	0.11

Winning Trades		Losing Trades	
Total Winners:	68	Total Losers:	273
Gross Profit:	$208,890	Gross Loss:	-$145,260
Average Win:	$3,072	Average Loss:	-$532
Largest Win:	$12,030	Largest Loss:	-$1,370
Largest Drawdown in Win:	-$495	Largest Peak in Loss:	$2,630
Avg Drawdown in Win:	-$80	Avg Peak in Loss:	$12
Avg Run Up in Win:	$4,087	Avg Run Up in Loss:	$12
Avg Run Down in Win:	-$80	Avg Run Down in Loss:	-$532
Most Consec Wins:	4	Most Consec Losses:	22
Ave # of Consec Wins:	1.24	Avg # of Consec Losses:	4.88
Avg # of Bars in Wins:	1.01	Avg # of Bars in Losses:	.03

Figure 2.1 Performance history of my short-term S&P 500 futures trading system with a $500 stop loss. Note the large number of consecutive losses (22) as well as the very low average profit per trade ($187). In addition, the 19.9 percent accuracy of this method using a $500 stop loss makes it essentially not tradable.

Now, let's examine the same system but with a stop loss of $3,500, one that is more realistic based on market volatility and historical price swings. Figure 2.2 shows these historical results.

SUMMARY

Overall			
Total Trades:	339	Winning Percentage:	68.7%
Average Trade:	$559	Payout Ratio (Avg Win/Loss):	0.68
Avg # of Bars in Trade:	1.16	Z-Score (W/L Predictability):	-1.2
Avg # of Trades per Year:	31.0	Percent in the Market:	13.0%
Max Closed-out Drawdown:	-$37,435	Max Intra-day Drawdown:	-$37,455
Account Size Required:	$54,773	Return Pct:	346%
Open Equity:	$0	Kelly Ratio:	0.2294
Current Streak:	6 wins	Optimal f:	0.31
Winning Trades		**Losing Trades**	
Total Winners:	233	Total Losers:	106
Gross Profit:	$567,753	Gross Loss:	-$378,245
Average Win:	$2,437	Average Loss:	-$3,568

Winning Trades (con't)		Losing Trades (con't)	
Largest Win:	$19,730	Largest Loss:	-$6,270
Largest Drawdown in Win:	-$3,395	Largest Peak in Loss:	$4,655
Avg Drawdown in Win:	$-684	Avg Peak in Loss:	$591
Avg Run Up in Win:	$3,304	Avg Run Up in Loss:	$591
Most Consec Wins:	20	Most Consec Losses:	5
Avg # of Consec Wins:	3.38	Avg # of Consec Losses:	1.56
Avg # of Bars in Wins:	1.32	Avg # of Bars in Losses:	.81

Figure 2.2 The same system with a $3,500 stop loss in S&P 500 futures. Note the dramatic differences in performance history compared to Figure 2.1. In particular note that while with a $500 stop loss the winning percentage is only 19.9%, with a $3,500 stop loss, it rises to 68.7%.

The rapid growth of electronic trading in stocks, commodities, and FOREX (foreign currency exchange) has opened many doors to trading opportunities. But not all doors lead to profits. Far too many of them lead to dead ends or losses. Market participants with a vested interest in separating speculators from their hard earned money have jumped on the electronic trading bandwagon in large numbers. There are many ways in which aspiring traders can lose money but precious few ways in which they can make money. No matter what the magazine and television advertisements may lead you to believe, profitable trading is neither easy to learn nor easy to achieve.

CHANGE VS. CONSTANCY

The underlying goal of all trading, whether short-term, long-term, or day trading, is to capitalize on changes in market trends. Powerful computers and sophisticated software programs have facilitated the development of numerous trading methodologies designed to recognize advantage of changes in market trends and to take advantage of them. In addition to the development of new trading methods, the ability to "back test" trading approaches has added vastly to our arsenal of trading tools. "Back testing" is looking at previous data and trying to fit a pattern, trend, or model to it that might help to predict the future. By implementing such an objective approach to a trading system and method evaluation, we have been able to identify what works and what does not. Most traders still use trading tools that, thanks to computer back testing, are either known to be unreliable or only marginally profitable.

Computer testing allows us to separate market myth from market reality. Only a handful of trading methods have shown themselves to be valid, while many others have no demonstrable efficacy. While underlying market conditions have changed, some profitable trading methods have persisted. The implementation of these basic methodologies, however, has required some changes, particularly in the area of evaluating risk. Adaptation to changes in market volatility is one of the keys to consistent profits as a day trader.

EXPLORING AND EXPLODING A MYTH

For years, new traders have been advised to "cut losses and let profits ride." As simple as this powerful rule may seem, it is, in reality, exceptionally difficult to apply because it lacks specificity. What exactly does it mean? How do we put this bit of incredible wisdom into practice?

To the vast majority of traders it means that the dollar risk they are willing to accept on a trade must be small in comparison to their potential profits. They translate this goal into their trading by using "small" stop losses. Their logic is that if they risk a relatively small amount on their trades then they stand to lose a relatively small amount when they are wrong. As I have demonstrated clearly in my previous examples (see Figures 2.1 and 2.2) that logic at first blush seems to be correct, but it is faulty because it fails to take into account the role of intra-day market volatility. In other words, market volatility (the amount of intra-day market movement) may be so large that the small stop loss will, due to the volatility, be triggered every day.

Let's take a practical example. If you decide to buy Intel shares at $15 with a average daily trading range of $14.50 to $15.50, and you set your stop loss at $14.98, you'll likely get stopped out repeatedly—the typical daily random movement or even the spread between the bid and offer price will get you stopped out over and over. The stop loss position needs to take into account the normal volatility of a security or commodity so that you at least have a chance to gain on the upward leg while still being protected from larger losses.

In the above example a more reasonable stop loss might be $2 which would be twice the average daily trading range. The inexperienced trader will balk at the stop loss, claiming that it's too high. The experienced trader will immediately realize the wisdom of using a stop loss that cannot be executed as a result of underlying "noise" or average trading range. Random market behavior is such that a small stop, rather than protect a trader, will actually hurt him or her. When a loss occurs it will be small but the stop loss will assure a loss virtually every time. Accuracy will decline, and the trading methodology will fail. We know from back testing as well as actually trading with different risk levels that larger stop losses lead to higher accuracy and larger profits.Yet another unintended consequence of the small stop loss is that the persistent losses will undermine the trader's psychology. His discipline will deteriorate, resulting in further losses. Eventually, trading capital will be depleted, and the game will be lost.

The adaptation of stop losses to market conditions is but one example of how trading methods must adapt to the times. Based upon actual experience as well as back testing, the following conditions now prevail:

1. Intra-day market volatility is now larger than ever before, so stop losses that were sufficient in the 1980s, 1990s, and early 2000s are no longer sufficient today. This volatility not only affects stop losses but also influences other variables in the trading system.
2. The size of the stop loss is only one of several variables that must be adjusted to account for market volatility.

In short, trading methods that have worked consistently for many years are likely to work well now and in the future; however, adjustments need to be made in the stop loss as well as other variables.

As the example above clearly illustrated, the use of a "large" stop loss is a critical variable in the performance of this trading methodology. The method was the same but the stop loss was different. The "small stop" simply does not work! Still, however, some day trading "experts" encourage traders to use small stop losses.

This simple illustration pinpoints only one of the numerous market myths that can either lead to losses or prevent profits. While volatility has created a need to adjust stop loss sizes higher, many traders are still encouraged by "old school" teachers and traders to use small stop losses. This book will alert you to similar pitfalls that have been perpetuated by market myths, and it will also guide you to effective and consistent trading approaches.

THE WEAKEST LINK IN THE CHAIN

Notwithstanding the importance of effective and consistent trading methodologies, there are other factors and forces that can denigrate performance or, in fact, lead to losses. Even the most profitable trading approach can be rendered useless in the hands of an undisciplined trader. I'll be honest: Clearly the weak link in the trading chain has always been and will always be the trader.

Traders are told that in order to achieve success they need to be disciplined. Here is yet another market myth or at best a misunderstanding. Hundreds of articles and at least several dozen books have been written about trader or investor psychology (several of which were authored by this writer). While these books offer solutions to the problems of poor trader discipline, I believe that there is a simple and very obvious solution that many of us overlook

Discipline in the absence of confidence is a hollow objective. Confidence in a trading methodology creates discipline. *Discipline is the result, not the cause.* It would be "normal" to lack confidence in a consistently losing trading approach. To have discipline when using such a flawed approach would be absurd. Discipline and confidence are created by profitable methodologies. Hence, by focusing on methods that work (i.e. create profits) we significantly increase confidence, which, in turn improves discipline. Hopefully the methods in this book will build confidence to help surmount the "weak link in the chain" syndrome.

DOES THIS BOOK GIVE ALL THE ANSWERS?

I'm not sure I've ever seen a book that has all the answers; indeed, I do not pretend to have all the answers to guaranteed successful trading in this book. But, in reality, there aren't that many answers to be found. My more than forty years of experience have taught me many valuable lessons. When distilled, they boil down to a few global truths. The validity and consistency of these cannot be denied if trading success, either as a position trader or a day trader, is to follow.

The fact is that trading, in the final analysis, is much simpler than many would have us believe, but paradoxically, in its simplicity it is complicated. Hopefully, this book will "cut to the chase," eliminating the complexity in order to reduce the answers to their most concise form. To this end, I believe that you will find the information that follows to be as *specific* as possible, as *objective* as possible, and as *clear* as possible. I want you to use this information to achieve your own independence as a day trader. I have no interest in fostering dependency even if you do value my opinions. Whether you subscribe to any of my informational services or not, I encourage you to make your own trading decisions within the context of your financial ability and risk tolerance. This book is intended to set you on the road to success, but it cannot teach you everything you need to know about day trading; you'll learn also from other sources and from your own experience.

Do I have all the answers for you? No. But as I described above, I do have a few solid and effective truths you can go forward with. In spite of my experience and my research, I constantly force myself to remember that all markets have a degree of inherent randomness. Such random behavior is more pronounced on the intra-day level than in any other time frame. It is the random behavior of markets that at one and the same time creates profitable opportunities but also annoys us, frustrates us, and sometimes limits our profits. When we have an understanding of the essential truths of trading, such events and errors start to make sense within a bigger context, and, with experience, we can learn, adapt, and amend our trading practices to achieve better results.

THERE ARE NO GUARANTEES

Traders want guarantees. I want guarantees. When I go to a doctor or a lawyer, I would love a guarantee that the doctor's treatment or the lawyer's advice is going to work every time. But sadly, that isn't the case. If I give you indicators, systems, and methods, their success depends on the weakest link in the chain. And that link, as I've indicated, is you.

One of the things my vast experience has taught me is that no matter how good a system or method may be, traders will often find ways to abuse, modify, or misuse them whether consciously or unconsciously. The end result of such misuse is usually a financial loss. But it goes much deeper than that. Misuse of methods and systems creates confusion and lack of direction. Confusion and lack of direction create losses. Losses undermine confidence. Lack of confidence gives growth to lack of discipline. Lack of discipline leads to further losses. Although I would love to give you guarantees, I can't and won't do that. Perfection isn't possible. I will, however, tell you that the methods are well worth the time you devote to studying and applying them.

ESSENTIAL TRUTHS

I sincerely believe that this book can be very beneficial to you provided you take the necessary time and effort to study my methods and systems. Remember, above all, that unless you have a solid structure and organization to your trading and investing there is no indicator, system, or method that will help you. Without the Setup, Trigger, and Follow-Through method (STF) I will present in Chapter 3, you will be lost in a sea of randomness, tossed about like a ship without a captain. And that will give you the same dismal results that most traders experience. Use this book as a reference guide. Study my methods. Apply them and see how they work for you.

Following are the basic skills you must master in order to achieve the best result as a trader:

Embrace Uncommon Thinking

To be successful you need to avoid common thinking—or you will experience common results. In markets these days—with their wild swings and jolts—the "common results" means that you will lose money. Why? First, because a good 90 percent of traders (or more) lose money. It's that simple. If you want to be a winner in the markets, then you must not engage in common thinking. It is also that simple.

What is common thinking? I will elaborate as we proceed.

Think and Act like a Pro

If you have been honest with yourself and have confessed to some of your limitations in life and in the marketplace, we can begin some preliminary work on how to improve your results and trade like a professional day trader. My work would not be complete if I provided you with nothing more than a series of market methods, indicators, and trading techniques. Because the trader is indeed the weakest link in the chain, I am compelled to discuss the psychological and behavioral aspects of day trading.

It all starts with embracing the idea that trading requires a professional mindset, attitude, and approach.

Get Organized

Organization is vital to the success of any venture. It is important to know where you are headed, when you expect to get there, and which vehicles you will use to reach your destination. Without organization, these tools can often be misplaced. Your charts, books, formulae, trading rules and telephone numbers, etc. must be readily available.

Effective day trading is not something that can be done from a spare corner of your house. You need an area that's devoted to this profession—one in which you can store the tools you'll need and where you won't be disturbed by ringing phones, barking dogs, and so forth.

Furthermore, you must block off in advance the time each day you will devote to trading. Be rigid about it. Don't let anything interrupt it—short of the house catching fire. The more organized you are, the greater your chances of successful day trading.

Develop Discipline

Being organized means being disciplined. This is, of course, easier said than done. Take a course on self-improvement, such as those offered by the Dale Carnegie Institute or the Anthony Robbins organization. You will learn that success requires discipline and that discipline can be learned. Discipline can often be improved through the simple application of behavioral learning techniques. My book, *The Investor's Quotient, 2nd ed.* (New York: John Wiley & Sons, 2000), gives specific suggestions and techniques designed to help you improve your self-discipline. In addition, there are many simple exercises that you can use.

Remember that discipline from one area of your life tends to be reflected in all others. If you lack the discipline to change such negative habits as excessive drinking, overeating, and smoking, then you will probably lack the discipline required for successful trading. You may need to overcome these habits first, or you may need to conquer all lapses of discipline at once.

Finally, know that being rigid in following rules is not necessarily a form of discipline. Being a disciplined trader also means being flexible enough to change course as soon as you see that the action you have taken is not working. The rigid trader will believe too strongly in his or her trading rules, and this can prove destructive. Disciplined traders learn and adapt. Trading is a game of probability and probability leaves no room for rigidity.

DEVELOP SIMPLE AND EFFECTIVE TRADING APPROACHES

One of the greatest barriers to success in trading is that systems become too complicated, too burdensome, or too time-consuming to use consistently. If you build a boat, make certain you can get it into the water. Once in the water, make certain it can move. Some boat builders have built their ships so big and so top heavy that upon being launched they slid straight to the bottom. Others make boats that, although they float, are cumbersome and hard to turn swiftly. Above all, your trading system must work and it must be able to rapidly respond to changes in the market.

Too many traders spend too much time developing complicated, sophisticated "trading systems" that are difficult to implement. In my experience, most successful futures traders use simple methods. Throughout this book, you will hear me repeat "Keep it simple" again and again.

If you keep it simple you will be less consumed with details, less troubled with self-discipline, and you will shorten your market response time. This alone will prove valuable. If it takes too long to figure out what your method is telling you to do, that's a bad sign. Therefore, keep it simple!

KEEP IMPULSIVE TRADING TO A MINIMUM—STAY RELATIVELY ISOLATED

There's a great deal to be said for isolationism in trading. In other words, in order to keep free of impulse, it is often best that you not know the news.

This sounds counterintuitive at first, since in many cases the market is driven by the news, even reacting on a minute-by-minute basis. The problem is that if you spend your time glued to the TV news channels, you're reacting as the market often does: randomly, impulsively, and often irrationally.

So turn off the news channel. Avoid the business news. Odds are that it won't help you. In fact, chances are that it will hurt you. Then you can "keep your head while all those around you are losing theirs." You will, in so doing, focus on following your system and avoid the costly errors that are frequently the result of impulsive behavior.

I favor isolation in order to achieve my goals. I prefer not to listen to the radio or television news, not to read the newspapers, not to listen to the opinions of others, and not to discuss the markets, even with other professionals. I do this because I know that I may have weaknesses. In order to be strong and avoid impulsive actions motivated by the emotions of fear and/or greed, I must limit my exposure to extraneous information. This general approach is especially important to the day trader.

This is my point of view, one that is not shared by many other day trading experts. They would have you believe that the successful day trader must constantly keep his or her finger on the pulse of the news, reacting and responding accordingly. Indeed there are two clear and distinct schools of thought in this respect.

The pure market technician will tell you that his or her methods of trading are sufficiently sensitive and accurate to trigger market entry prior to a news event. The theory behind the assertion is that insiders know the news before the news is revealed to the general public. Given this knowledge they enter positions before the news is released. When the news hits the street and the markets react, insiders exit their position. Therein lies the logic in the "buy on anticipation, sell on realization" or "buy the rumor, sell the fact." Odds are that this point of view is correct.

The technical day trader (or short-term trader) believes that the technical indicators he uses will reflect insider activity prior to release of the news. As a result, as a day trader it may actually be detrimental to listen to and react to the news as it becomes public knowledge (you may be reacting too late).

The other school of thought is that when news is released the markets may react quickly and often with a large move. If you are quick enough to climb aboard a move and to exit that move before it reverses you could profit substantially. I agree.

The good news is that such moves do occur and that they are quite frequent. The bad news is that they are often so quick that exceptional agility is required if one wants to capture profits as a day trader. At times these moves can begin and end in the course of several minutes or less. In Chapter 7 I will discuss at least one method, Volatility Breakout, that can help you take advantage of such moves in the day time frame.

Clearly the two approaches presented above are not mutually exclusive. There is a place for both although my preference is for the purely technical method as opposed to methods that respond to or are tied to news.

PLAN YOUR TRADES AND TRADE YOUR PLANS

This market cliché is just as true today as when it was coined. It is the best way to avoid the vast majority of day trades. If you are prepared, and if you act according to your plan, you will have taken the first and most important step to practicing self-discipline. Without a doubt this is easier said than done. If, however, your methods and indicators are part of a clear trading model such as my STF (Setup, Trigger, and Follow-Through) plan, the probability of errors is substantially reduced. Remember, there's nothing telling you that you have to make a trade.

KEEP YOUR OBJECTIVES CLEARLY IN MIND

You must always keep your goals in mind. If you are a short-term trader, then you must think and act like one. However, if you're a long-term trader, then your perception of the markets and your corresponding actions must be consistent with these objectives. If you are a day trader, then your goal will be to enter and exit positions within the course of a day (however we choose to define the term "day"). I have found it best to have a list of objectives and goals handy for quick reference in times of need.

DEAL EFFECTIVELY WITH STRESS; VENT YOUR FRUSTRATIONS

Don't "live the markets." In other words, don't become so wrapped up in what you're doing that you lose track of your own stress level and start making decisions with your gut instead of your head. In order to improve market decisions, it is necessary that you deal effectively with tension. You need to recognize that day trading is an inherently stressful activity and take steps accordingly.

There are many ways you can do this. Exercise is one good way to cope with stress. It can help you vent frustrations and give you a chance to get your mind off the markets. If possible, set up a place in your house where you can exercise—whether on a treadmill, a weight machine, or something else. If there's no such place available, join a gym or take an aerobics class. If nothing else, take a long walk at the end of each trading day. It will help clear the cobwebs from your brain and prepare you for the next day.

Find something to do that's as different as possible from trading and fit it into your schedule.

- Discover a hobby.
- Attend a concert.
- Join a book club.
- Walk through a museum.

The point is to find something that's non-stressful, non-goal oriented, and non-competitive, to give those parts of your mind a chance to relax.

Leave the markets at the office or at your trading desk. The role of stress, particularly as it applies to the day trader, cannot and should not be minimized. The more you day trade the more stress you will have. The more markets you day trade the greater will be your tension levels. The larger your position, the larger your stress. It's a very simple fact.

Stress in and of itself is a natural response to pressure and the threat of losses, but it is particularly important if it results in faulty trading decisions. If you plan to day trade as your profession, then regular and effective stress reduction must be a significant part of your plan.

KEEP COMMISSION COSTS LOW

My broker friends and associates will not be pleased with what I have to tell you in this section—but say it I must. As a day trader, your overhead consists of losses, your information technology infrastructure, and commissions.

Losses are a subject we'll discuss as we go forward. Your IT infrastructure can and should be inexpensive; essentially anyone with a good, fast computer can day trade effectively. Here I want to discuss commission costs.

Commissions are really a built-in loss factor. Together with poor order execution they constitute a significant cost of doing business. Poor order fills and commissions can eat up about 25 percent of your profits before your very eyes. Since day traders often operate on a fairly small profit margin, it is even more important for you to save as much money as possible on all operating costs. The largest and most costly of these is commissions.

Some traders who want and need the advice of brokers will need to do business with a "full-service house." They will, therefore, pay higher commissions. There's nothing wrong with this provided it is cost-effective. If you deal with a full-service house and pay higher commissions, it doesn't necessarily mean you will fail.

However, you must get some return for what you are paying in higher costs. If you do not get a return, then you're not making a sound business decision. If you day trade actively without the need of advice or information, then you are entitled to lower commissions. You can ask your full-service broker for a discount. Depending on how often you trade and the service you want, commission costs can be as low as a few dollars or as high as $100 per round turn. Some options brokers have charged even more, particularly when they know that a new client has no idea of how much he or she should pay.

Be informed about their discount policies. Don't be afraid to ask how much trading you will need to do in order to benefit from the commission break. Run the numbers.

Finally, if you see that you are not using any of the information put out by the house you're dealing with, take the time to investigate another house offering lower commissions. But first, since a good broker/trader relationship is very important, ask your current broker if he or she can lower his or her rates. If that's possible, well and good. If not, you'll need to shop around for something less expensive.

I can't overemphasize enough that one of the keys to successful trading is holding down your costs. The better you get at this, the better your profitability ratio.

AVOID OVER-TRADING

One of the greatest secrets to success in day trading is to avoid the temptation to "over-trade." This is true in all types of trading. Far too many traders adhere to the erroneous assumption that you must be in every market at all times. There is no substance or truth to this belief. As a matter of fact, market professionals prefer to concentrate on certain markets and only on certain types of moves.

You cannot and should not be in all markets at all times. You are better off trading on quality as opposed to quantity. You are also better off trading larger positions in fewer markets as opposed to smaller positions on many markets. A day trader can only manage positions in a limited number of markets at the same time. If you over-trade, it will only be a matter of time before you begin to miss signals and trading opportunities. In day trading less may be more, and the ability to say "no" is important.

To sum up, here are Bernstein's Basic Rules for traders:

1. Get organized. Mark out a time and a place for your trading and insist on its sanctity. This is your spot to make money; don't let other people or their stuff invade it.
2. Be disciplined. Success in any field depends on your ability to stay focused and get the job done. Day trading is no different. In fact it probably demands more self-discipline than many other professions.
3. Build a simple trading system. Complications are not your friends. Your system should be simple and flexible, able to swiftly respond to market changes. If it's too cumbersome, it will quickly lead you into distress.
4. Avoid trading on impulse. Get a strategy and stick to it. Sometimes impulse trades can work; more often they lose money and lead to panic.
5. Plan your trades with clear objectives. The stronger your strategic approach to day trading, the better your chances of profit. Each move you make should fit into your overall plan, designed to advance you toward your goal.
6. Deal with your stress level. Allowing tension to build up inside you is a recipe for disaster. Rather than ignore it, find a way to structure your day so you can vent stress and approach your trading in a good frame of mind.
7. Keep overhead costs down. Especially keep an eye on commission costs. If you're getting worthwhile advice from

your broker, well and good. But you should constantly evaluate if the cost is worth the counsel.

8. Shun over-trading. You can't be in all places at once. Nor should you try to be. Choose your markets carefully and stay in them. No matter how tempting things look in another market, don't enter it unless it's part of your strategic plan.

RECAP

In order to be successful as a day trader in the stock or futures markets, you will need to cultivate certain behaviors while eliminating others. Identifying your strengths and weaknesses and learning the steps toward developing a winning attitude and repertoire are the building blocks of success in all forms of trading; however, they are especially critical in day trading.

Chapter **3**

An Overview of Day Trading Markets and Methods

Before proceeding into specific and illustrated day trading tools and techniques, it's worth a few moments to develop the larger context. We need to know more about the different markets to trade in (there are many more choices than there were just a few years ago). Each market has its own characteristics and suitability to different types and styles of trading. I'll give a brief overview of what makes a good market to trade and a list of my favorite "products" in those markets. With this discussion in mind, I'll introduce my favorite trading techniques.

WHICH MARKETS ARE BEST FOR DAY TRADING?

This is a substantive question, the responses to which can easily make the difference between success and failure. Many markets are suitable for short-term trades or as investments, but there are relatively few markets that support effective day trading. Here are a few simple rules and characteristics that should be considered in selecting markets for day trading.

MARKETS SHOULD BE ACTIVE

Day traders should trade active markets only (that is, markets with securities that have enough participants and volume to provide the movement and transparency to make data-based judgments and to get timely and natural order executions). Traders should pick the active securities within those markets. Most commodity, stock, and FOREX markets qualify.

Generally speaking, I prefer stocks that trade on average at least 2 million shares daily and commodities that trade at least 5,000 contracts daily. The more active the market, the more likely you are to show positive results. Lack of liquidity (i.e., low volume) will result in bad price executions as well as potential difficulty in entry and exit of positions. The more active the market, the better historical information you have on which to base your trades.

MARKETS SHOULD HAVE SUBSTANTIAL TRADING RANGES

Trade markets that have reasonably good daily trading ranges. In other words, a market could very well be actively traded but it may have very limited movement within the course of a typical day. I prefer to trade stocks with a minimum daily range of 50 cents (that is, difference between the daily high and low) but preferably in the $1 to $2 area or even higher.

When the average daily trading range is very small (e.g., 50 cents for a stock) you will need to compensate for the small range by trading a larger number of shares in order to make the venture worthwhile. Within the commodities markets, I prefer a $200 daily trading range. These ranges should not only be large enough to profit but consistent over the days, weeks, and months. However, it should be noted that in times of great economic upheaval, daily ranges may be much larger than normal for many stocks.

MARKETS SHOULD NOT HAVE TOO MUCH VOLATILITY

While a wide trading range is better than a narrow one in both stocks and commodities, it is also true that a large trading range can be too risky for traders. For example, the Natural Gas futures market in late 2008 had some daily trading ranges of over $4,000. To many traders such a large daily trading range is too risky. The full sized S&P 500 futures contract can trade in a daily range of $10,000 per day or more. In such cases, trading the E-Mini S&P futures contract, which is one-fifth the size of the full S&P 500, is more suitable to many traders. Why? Because very large trading ranges are indicative of large volatility, which in turn suggests large risks. Large volatility is not the best situation for traders who cannot afford the risk of large price swings.

There is no rule of thumb for this; it depends on your own risk tolerance. Also, a market that has become much more volatile in a recent time period may suggest that the economy itself is due for a change in fundamentals. In that case, clearly, investors of all kinds face increased risk, none more so than day traders. So while a good range is important, consistency over time is even more important.

CHARACTERISTICS OF MARKETS FOR DAY TRADING

Because market conditions change over time and the markets noted above may not always be the best candidates for day trading, here is a brief synopsis of what to look for when selecting the best markets for day trading:

Sufficient trading volume. Activity should be sufficient for you to have ease of market entry and exit at reasonably good prices.

Volatility. The trading range of a market or stock should be sufficiently large to provide ample opportunities for profit.

Primary market in a sector leadership. The stock or commodity should be a leader, the primary or most active market in that complex. If you are considering the use of a stock or commodity market that is part of a larger sector (i.e., soybeans in the soybean complex or a biotechnology stock in the biotechnology sector) then choose the primary or most active market in that complex. As an example, you would use soybeans in the soybean complex, or crude oil in the energy complex, or the most active stock in the biotechnology sector.

With these characteristics in mind, here are the types of markets I generally favor.

FUTURES MARKET FAVORITES

I do a lot of trading in futures markets. There are many reasons; an important one is that there is no "human factor" headline risk—a crooked accounting firm cannot be caught cooking the books for gold, oil, or corn. Within the futures markets are several securities representing baskets of stocks, such as the S&P 500 and the E-Mini version of it. While these don't completely eliminate "human factors" risks, they are largely minimized.

The specific futures markets I currently favor for day trading are as follows (not necessarily in order of preference):

- S&P 500 and E-Mini S&P 500 futures
- E-Mini Russell futures
- NASDAQ and E-Mini NASDAQ futures
- 30-Year Treasury Bond and 10-Year Treasury notes futures
- Crude oil futures
- Gold futures
- All active currency futures and FOREX
- Soybean futures
- Corn futures

Importantly, I don't limit my trading to U.S. markets. Overseas markets are almost as easy to trade these days as domestic markets, and the same models and approaches generally work. In the European futures markets I include the Bund, Schatz, DAX, and FTSE as the primary markets for day trading.

The best day-trading candidates for stocks are those with sufficiently large volume to permit entry and exit within a penny or two of the current trading price. I prefer to day trade stocks that have been trading about 5 million shares daily on average.

You should make your decisions about which markets in which to day trade based on how much risk you can take. All too often, day traders take risks that are much too large for their accounts. They mistakenly assume that since they are "only" day trading that their risk will be limited. While it's true that their risk will be limited in terms of time their risk is unlimited in terms of price.

Having said this I am not suggesting that these are the only markets that are viable for day trading. These are my favorites. I believe that they offer the best opportunities for success with my methods as described in this book.

In addition to futures trading, many traders also trade the FOREX (foreign currency) markets. There are many popular currency "pairs." My methods will work in the FOREX market as long as you use the popular pairs such as the Swiss, Eurocurrency, British pound, yen, Australian dollar, and Canadian dollar versus the U.S. dollar and the cross relationships between these such as the Swiss versus the Euro, the Euro versus the yen, and so forth. Since the popularity and trading volume in the currency pairs may change in the future it is best to keep informed of these changes.

In stocks I recommend trading only active stocks as well as active ETFs.

APPLYING METHODS TO MARKETS

Having chosen your market in which to trade, you must now decide upon the appropriate vehicle and method for your day trading. The methods in this book are effective in stocks, futures, or FOREX. Given that the length of a "day" in each of these market sectors can differ markedly, you will need to make some adjustments in how you apply the methods. Before you make any trades based on what is contained herein, be certain that you are aware of and informed of the risks.

Here is a general description of each approach. We will discuss these in much more detail in the coming chapters.

THIRTY-MINUTE BREAKOUT FOR DAY TRADING S&P 500

This method is used exclusively in S&P futures using index behavior within the first thirty minutes of the day. Trades and trade criteria are setup during this time frame. Signals are generated in the full S&P 500 contract, and trades can be taken in the E-Mini S&P.

This method generally involves lower risk, given the smaller size of the contracts, but at the same time promises lower profit potential per trade.

GAP DAY TRADING

Gap day trades have enjoyed a long history of consistency. This method is not only one of the easiest to understand but also one of the most simple to implement. I have added some important rules and triggers to the gap day trade in order to improve accuracy and profitability. This trade is the subject of Chapter 5. Generally, the risk of gap trading using my methods is lower than other types of day trading methods. As in the case of all my methods you will always have a generally good idea of risk before you enter a gap trade.

SWING TRADING WITH CHANNEL AND CONFIRMATION

This method uses the moving average channel (MAC), which is a very useful trend and timing indicator. Swing trading can be used very effectively for day trading by buying at support in an up trend and selling short at resistance in a down trend. It's discussed further in Chapter 6. The risk of trading the channel is a function of the channel size. You will always have a very close idea of your risk before you enter a channel trade.

SHORT-TERM DIVERGENCE WITH THE STF METHOD

I have developed a method for identifying and implementing divergence patterns which, when combined with Trigger and Follow-Through are excellent day trading tools. These will be explained and discussed in Chapters 9, 10, and 11 with specific entry and exit strategies for the day trader. The risk level of a divergence trade is determined by the configuration of the divergence size. You will always know how much your risk will be, and you will therefore have the choice of either rejecting a trade or finding a less risky vehicle for the trade.

These methods work well in some markets and may work in all markets, depending on your risk tolerance, size of trade, understanding of the market, and your trading objectives. Keep in mind that *any* method of day trading, if it is to be successful, must include the following features:

1. Profit maximizing strategies. These are a pivotal factor in day trading.
2. Entry and exit strategies. It's key to know when to get in and when to get out.

I will discuss all these methods in greater detail as we proceed. Based on that discussion, you can decide which of them are appropriate for you, depending on your risk tolerance and which markets you intend to trade in. But keep in mind that you are not limited to merely one of these methods. All can be successful in the hands of the skilled day trader.

TECHNICAL ANALYSIS

The methods listed above rely to one extent or another on technical analysis. By this term, we mean the mathematical or "pattern" analysis of security price behavior and various indicators thereof. It is a prominent, but not the only, analytical approach to day trading.

Technical analysis is largely done by observing and mathematically analyzing patterns that occur in the markets. The tools used in analysis range from the simple, like ordinary regression, to the highly complex, such as statistical tools reminiscent of those used in data mining. Such tools are used to build models of everything from consumer preferences to crimes to military targets.

But technical analysis isn't just about the numbers; it is really about "fitting" a pattern to the collective buying and selling behavior in the markets. We should never forget that at bottom, the market is made up of thousands upon thousands of investors, buying and selling. Thus in the end, technical analysis is about measuring and describing the behavior and the consistency of behavior of a crowd.

HISTORICAL BACK TESTING

Traders like to test and develop their indicators and methods. With a powerful computer, historical price data, and an effective back-testing software program, it's possible, by using optimizing programs, to create performance histories for stocks. Such back testing must be approached carefully. Because back testing looks at past performance it can lose sight of factors that will affect stock performance in the future. Often these can't be foreseen, and a stock that has performed well in the past will hit a roadblock in the future. Basing all your day trading decisions on back testing can be a highly risky method—a bit like driving by looking in the rear view mirror.

Traders can test trading parameters against historical data to see which of these parameters work best. Such testing is referred to as *optimization.*

Unless a trading system has been developed with a minimum of optimization, the odds are that it will fail in the future. To complicate the theory, ideas about what constitutes minimal optimization vary from one trader to another.

Can we develop good trading systems and methods with back testing and optimization? Indeed we can, provided that the rules of implementation (i.e., entry and exit) are specific, objective, operational, and programmable. But does such an approach get us what we want?

I suggest that when it comes to day trading, a totally mechanical approach may not be the most effective procedure. Those who are familiar with my work on position trading systems (i.e., not day trading) or who have read my previous books on day trading may be somewhat surprised by what I am about to say. I believe that profitable day trading must combine an operational and objective entry method with an operationally based but not entirely mechanical exit strategy.

TESTING THE TOOLS IN THIS BOOK

Traders who have access to system-testing software will likely want to back test the indicators and methods discussed in this book. In so doing there is a tendency to ignore the Trigger and Follow-Through components of the methods.

Back testing and optimization help you understand the market pattern to Set-Up the trade. They're far less helpful in showing how to fire off the trade and manage it once made. Given that Follow-Through is an integral aspect of my suggested trading methods and that Follow-Through is not completely mechanical, the results from back testing may either understate or overstate what your actual experience may be with my methods.

Furthermore, the methods suggested in this book are specific to given markets. If a trader attempts to apply the methods to markets that are too thinly traded, the results may not be helpful in assessing the reliability of the method.

My advice to you is to evaluate the methods as you learn them. Go through a number of "paper trades" (i.e., simulated trades) using various profit maximizing strategies and decide for yourself which approach works best for you. A computer back test will not necessarily give you the correct information.

Remember that every method must be evaluated within the context of the Set-Up, Trigger, and Follow-Through structure that I will explain in detail. Unless a method can be evaluated within the context of this structure, you will not have sufficient information to make an intelligent decision about its efficacy or appropriateness for your account and risk.

THE IMPORTANCE OF OBJECTIVITY

The goal of the day trader is to end each day with as much profit as possible. The day trader must therefore adjust to changing market conditions once a trade is in process. Note that I advocate strict adherence to entry rules and triggers but less rigid methods of exit. While market entry is clear, objective, and specific, I believe that market exits are more flexible as a function of the need to maximize profits on each and every day trade.

I have found that the way we profitably exit day trades (and, for that matter, all trades) can be the critical variable in determining our success or failure. I cannot overemphasize the importance of having and using a profit-maximizing strategy that is intertwined with your exit strategy.

There are several possible exit strategies that can be used. While I have attempted to make these as objective and as operational as possible, there is a certain element of experience and decision-making that is necessary for them to work at their best. At times the process is not entirely objective. Some readers will take issue with this aspect of my work since it is not purely objective and cannot be back tested. For this I offer apologies in advance. In my defense I will say that within this book you will find methods that I believe are more objective and operational than virtually anything else that is available today for day traders.

To clarify the discussion that follows, here are some working definitions:

Trading method: a compilation of entry and exit tools consisting of a Set-Up, Trigger, and Follow-Through approach wherein there is flexibility in the exit strategy. This book will explain the STF approach in the next chapter and show you several trading methods in the chapters that follow.

Trading system: a completely objective trading method with a specific and operational exit strategy (i.e., one that is not subject to user opinion or input). Typically trading systems are computerized and may be "wired in" to the extent that they automatically place orders. This book is not about trading systems. It is about trading methods, timing indicators, triggers, and exit strategies.

Timing indicator: a timing indicator is a tool that provides us with information about a change in market trend or a pending change in market trend. A timing indicator, as it is used by most traders, is a call to action. It supposedly tells us when to buy or sell. My STF structure uses timing triggers as part of the process but we never use triggers without an associated set-up.

It is my belief that day trading has a scientific basis as well as a set of rules that are objective and operational. The rules are clear and not subject to interpretation. That being said, I must add that there is also a certain level of experience and judgment that must be achieved in order to be truly successful as a day trader. We could easily fall into a lengthy discussion as to whether it is experience or instinct that separates the very profitable day trader from her marginally profitable counterpart. Let's not go down that road.

DAY TRADING MYTHS

Be careful what you tell yourself . . . You may start believing it
Be careful what others tell you . . . You may start believing it.

As a day trader studies the highly sophisticated back testing and optimization tools, it is easy to succumb to the belief that these tools will do everything and solve all problems. But they don't. *They are tools; you are the trader.* You must learn how to use the tools and benefit from what they do, but they won't do all the work nor will they make the decisions for you.

The good news about day trading in this age of precision charting and powerful computers is that there are fully objective and quantifiable methods available to us. The bad news is that, in spite of these very effective tools, traders still wallow in the ignorance of subjective methods. There are many myths about day trading and the markets—and more in a period of high volatility. Don't fall for them.

Above all, you must avoid the myth that the tool will do everything; but you must also avoid assuming that tools and methods are unimportant. Like tools in the hands of any skilled craftsman, the tools of day trading make it possible for you to create a strong and profitable series of trades. It's a question of balance and proportion. The better you get to know these tools and methods, the better you'll become at using them; the more you'll know about their strengths and limits.

Avoid unrealistic claims about the available tools; they are sold hard with lots of hype, and if you don't know how to use them, or if they don't apply well to the type of trading you do, you'll run into problems.

Here is a list of the worst common myths about short-term trading and day trading:

Small stop losses will protect me. As I've shown in the charts in Chapter 2, an unrealistic stop loss can result in a less profitable day of trading. You must find the appropriate stop loss for your market and for your level of risk.

The more I day trade, the more money I will make. If you don't know what you're doing and start losing money, making more trades based on the same method is foolish. Albert Einstein once said, "Insanity is doing the same thing over and over again and expecting different results." That applies to day trading and short-term trading.

I need to make $XX a day. Setting an artificial target for your profit, whether gross or net, can psychologically hamper you in your trading. In coping with highly volatile markets, you need a maximum of flexibility.

I need to know the news in order to day trade. I've dealt with this issue in Chapter 2. Some knowledge of news trends is helpful, since the market is often news-driven. But it's not essential.

A bigger and faster computer will help me make more money. Any competent day trader or short-term trader can trade using a good, standard PC. Faster doesn't automatically equal more money—especially if you don't have a good grasp of the basics of trading.

Day trading S&P is the best game in town. There are other markets to trade that offer less risk and less volatility than S&P futures. S&P futures isn't the only game in town, and it's not necessarily the best game.

The FOREX market is the best market for day trading. FOREX trading can be very risky. When you trade FOREX you are competing with the biggest banks and the best currency traders in the world. Is that what you really want to do?

If I follow what the professional traders are doing, I'll succeed. Professional traders are grappling with the same problems and issues as you face. They're using the same tools and often the same methods. But ultimately, you're the only one who should make decisions about when and how to trade. The more confident you get in day trading, the more self-assured you'll feel in standing apart from the pros and building your own track record of trading.

MARKET MYTHS

In addition to the general myths about day trading that I have outlined above, there are a number of what I will term "market myths."

What exactly do I mean by "market myth"? Simply stated, traders have long believed that certain market patterns and or behaviors are valid indicators on which to make decisions. The fact of the matter is that most of these relationships simply do not hold up as valid when examined over a lengthy historical database. Several examples of what I have defined as market myths are:

1. **The "daily price reversal" pattern.** When a stock or commodity market drops below its previous daily low but closes above its previous daily close, a "reversal" is said to have occurred. The implication is that a trend change has taken place and that the trader should buy. My historical studies suggest that there is no predictive value to this pattern. The same holds true to a daily reversal down. In this case a stock or commodity trades above its previous daily high and closes below its previous daily close. The belief is that this pattern signals a top and the start of a down trend. As in the case of the daily reversal up, the pattern does not appear to be valid.

2. **"Turn Around Tuesday."** This is a popular but supported belief held by many traders. They argue that if prices have been moving down, they are likely to turn higher on Tuesday or vice versa if they have been moving lower. I have not found any valid statistical support for this pattern.

3. **Buy on a close above the fifty-day moving average.** Here is yet another market myth that does not hold water statistically. I will give you clear statistical evidence later in this book with regard to the accuracy of moving averages as timing triggers.

I mention these three as prominent examples of market myths. There are many others that have, in my view, led many traders down the primrose path. The question naturally arises why traders continue to believe in and use such ineffective tools—particularly since there is no objective evidence to support them. The answer is simple. As a group, traders tend to be lazy and unwilling to do their own work. Some of them would much rather take solace in market myths than do their own work. (I am certain that no one reading this book falls into the "lazy trader" category.)

DEBUNKING THE DAY-TRADING LIES

I have previously discussed the importance of being a realist when it comes to day trading. The fact of day trading is that it is neither as simple nor as easy as many would have us believe, nor is it as difficult as others would claim. My suggestion is that you avoid having unrealistic expectations for your day trading venture, whether these be on one extreme or the other. Simple works best, and consistency facilitates success. In order to begin your trip to successful day trading you will need to keep your eyes and ears open in order to separate truth from lies.

There has been an explosion of day trading information, services, newsletters, hotlines, courses, seminars, webinars, and trading systems. The claims range from the outlandish to the misleading. To a great extent we have the Internet to thank for this state of affairs. Be careful what you believe. Take the time to examine all the claims before you put any of your hard earned money into buying any course, system, or method.

I urge you to rid yourself of the above common market myths as well as others you may encounter. They will not serve you well. Rather than place your faith in the subjective and mythological, place your beliefs in objective methods such as those described herein. Take confidence from them, and continue to test your assertions. Constantly evaluate your risk tolerance and your understanding of methods and tools.

AVOIDING THE PITCH

In addition, it is important that you avoid the unrealistic claims that are so common in day trading. Successful traders recognize a pitch as a pitch and learn the truth through experience and hard work. Tools are only as good as the person using them. And as I've said above, technology isn't the solution; your skills and confidence are.

A "black box" panacea is just that—a panacea. It will sound good and feel good when it's installed on your computer, but the results will be below expectations and you'll have spent a lot of money on it. Here are some things to think about as you move forward into trading and set up your own methods of trading. Use them to boost your confidence.

- **Many traders are uneducated.** The simple reality of the day trading game is that thousands of aspiring traders are attracted to the lure of profits but they enter the game lacking skills, knowledge, and methods. Lack of education in day trading will hurt your ego as well as your pocketbook. Being an educated trader—and reading this book will make you one—immediately puts you in the upper 30 percent of all traders.

- **Many traders believe what the advertising says.** You're not one of them. You believe only what you can see and experience based either on your own trading or on your own testing.

- **Trading is a "zero sum game."** By this I mean that there is a winner for every loser. Every dollar you make is a dollar someone else lost. It's very simple. Day trading is the most challenging aspect of the zero sum game. You will do well to remember that every trader is your competitor. Your competitors want your money. Survival in the trading game, and in particular the day trading game, is for the fittest. As an educated and confident trader, you can triumph over your competitors.

From this point on, we get more specific. First I will discuss the Setup–Trigger–Follow-Through, or STF trading framework in Chapter 4; then I will cover specific trading techniques and thought processes you should know about.

But before turning to that, I want to reiterate what I have said in these early chapters: Success at day trading depends on you. It is your education, confidence, and adherence to the methods found in this book that will carry you through.

Chapter **4**

The Importance of Structure and the STF Framework

Question: What is structure and why is it vital to

success in trading?

Answer: It is a process, and it gives traders a sequence,

a structure to follow. Without that, traders lose

the discipline, focus, and consistency necessary to

proceed. For too many day traders, trading becomes a

random set of responses to the various stimuli in the

marketplace.

BUILDING A ROCK SOLID FOUNDATION

Lack of an underlying foundation and structure to trading is a leading cause of trading losses. Given that fact, it behooves us to explore one such structure under which all of the trading methods in this book will be executed. In other words, a trading structure is not only a set of specific steps but a set of procedures as well. Within each step there are specific procedures that must be completed if your trading is to be successful.

Furthermore, a trading structure will allow you to distinguish between methodological error and human error. Using a trading model enhances profits and minimizes losses by forcing the trader to employ a systematic and objective procedure.

THE SET-UP, TRIGGER, AND FOLLOW-THROUGH METHOD (STF)

The structure or trading model that I have developed over the years is called Setup, Trigger, and Follow-Through, or the STF framework. If you are familiar with my writings and teachings then you may already be familiar with STF. If so, you can skip this chapter. If you are not familiar with my STF then please continue to read what follows.

The STF trading structure is simple yet powerful. It requires that every trade, whether a day trade or longer, contain three elements that are critical to profitable trading. Here is a detailed description of the three elements of STF.

SET-UP (S)

A Set-Up is an identifiable pattern in the market. A pattern is defined as the tendency of a market to behave in certain ways either at given times or in response to given events. As an example, we know that the first two weeks of April tends to be a bullish time for stocks. The accuracy of this pattern can be verified by examining historical data. We also know that certain market relationships such as the one between price and the Momentum indicator (to be discussed) have relatively predictable outcomes. There are literally thousands of patterns in the markets but there are relatively few that are sufficiently reliable to be used as part of our structure. Many traders are familiar with patterns. Among those in which they have been educated are:

- Trendlines
- Reversals
- Day reversals
- Island tops and bottoms
- Head-and-shoulders tops and bottoms
- Flags
- Pennants
- Triangles

These patterns date back to the original work on technical analysis by Edwards and McGee and Graham and Dodd. Many of these patterns make sense but in historical testing and in actual results, they are not as reliable as one would have hoped. Nor are they as reliable as their proponents claim. If we add a

Trigger to these patterns, however, they become more reliable. I will discuss this point shortly.

Less traditional patterns that some traders classify as arcane, mythical, or mystical include the following:

- Elliott Wave
- Fibonacci
- Gann
- Percentage retracements and other types of "market geometry"

Japanese Candlestick formations have also gained popularity in recent years; however, there is a dearth of hard evidence to support the belief that they are sufficiently reliable or profitable.

Patterns are sometimes said to be divided into cycles and seasonals, both related to time-based repetition. Organizations such as the Foundation for the Study of Cycles have contributed a considerable body of evidence to strongly support both the existence as well as the reliability of the cycles and seasonals division. My own extensive research has validated the existence and persistence of seasonality in the stock and commodity markets, and I will provide some examples of seasonality later in this book

As traders looking for consistent methods, we must find reliable patterns on which to base our set-ups no matter what time frame we are using. If we begin our process with a reliable and predictable pattern then we significantly increase our odds of success, particularly when we combine a valid set-up with a trigger and a follow-through.

In summary, if we begin with a valid setup or pattern, then we begin with a strong base of reliability. The stronger our base of reliability, the more likely we are to produce trading profits. As noted above, there are many types of setups. I will show you several of these as we proceed.

TRIGGER (T)

In the STF model, a trigger (T) is a timing indicator that increases the probability of a trade based on the setup. In effect, a trigger verifies the fact that the market is moving in the direction predicted by the setup. Traders use a variety of traditional timing tools. These include:

- Moving averages
- Momentum
- Average Directional Index (ADX)
- Relative Strength Indicator (RSI)

These indicators are more effective when they are used in conjunction with a set-up or market pattern. A trigger simply confirms that a market is doing what it should be doing based on the set-up pattern.

There are hundreds of possible timing tools. They vary from the logical to the absurd and from the mathematical to the astrological. Sadly, many timing tools used by traders are based either on myth, faith, folklore or fantasy. Later I will provide a specific example of how the application of a trigger works within the STF structure.

FOLLOW-THROUGH (F)

The follow-through is the process to manage the trade when it is placed, that is, how long to hold on to it and when and how to terminate it. Follow-through is aimed to maximize the profit of the trade and to minimize its downside risk.

This is, in my view, the single most important aspect of the trading model. Even a mediocre trading method can become profitable if losses are kept to a minimum and profits are maximized. These two elements are, therefore, essential in the formula for trading success. Without a profit-maximizing strategy to buffer the small or medium-sized losses, the net result will be either a small losing proposition at best or a large losing proposition at worst. The day trader is particularly vulnerable to this limitation since, by definition, he or she must be out of all trades by the end of the day. This places a specific limit on how long a trade can be held.

We know that the bigger market moves take time to develop. It is for this reason that I support a mechanical or strictly rule-based approach to entering day trades but a less rigid, more situation-related method for exiting day trades. I'll discuss this in considerable detail when I give you detailed exit strategies. These strategies will take profit maximization into consideration.

Before going any further I would like to emphasize the critically important role of profit-maximizing strategies in the follow-through aspect of my STF structure or, for that matter, in any trading based on any methodology. The big money in trading is made in the big move, that is, a large change in the price of the financial instrument in a favorable direction. As day traders we are limited in how big a move we can capture simply because we are forced to exit at the end of the trading day. *It is critically important to maximize profits within the day time frame.* Without a profit maximizing strategy your day trading will be doomed to failure unless you have surgical timing and high accuracy. It is not unusual for the average trader to have numerous small winning trades only to give all the profits or more back with one losing trade. You must avoid this at all costs or your efforts at day trading will be totally wasted.

AN EXAMPLE OF HOW STF WORKS

Let us now take a look at an example of the STF approach in the S&P 500 futures market. Rest assured that we will look at many more detailed examples in the pages that follow.

> **Set-Up:** For the purpose of this example we will consider the Momentum indicator as the Set-Up method. The Momentum indicator is an effective tool for determining when prices are in an up trend or in a down trend and when the trend is likely to be changing. When Momentum rises above zero, it sets the market up for a move to the upside and when momentum falls below, it sets the market for a move to the downside. This will be the Set-Up condition that we will be using.

> **Trigger:** The Trigger to confirm a day trade buy will be a thirty-minute ending price above the high of the last thirty-minute price bar (or candlestick), or high/low range within a thirty-minute interval. The sell Trigger will be a thirty-minute ending price below the low of the last price bar. Note that this is merely an example and not specifically recommended as a

trading strategy. A variation on the theme of this approach will be presented later as a recommended strategy.

Follow-Through: The stop loss will be a reversal signal, and the profit target will be simple and twofold:

1. Exit at end of day or
2. Trail stop loss once position is profitable

By the term "trailing stop" we mean "a stop that is moved repeatedly to reflect market conditions for the purpose of capturing as large a profit as possible." In other words, the stop moves upward in accordance with the stock price as it rises, to preserve the gain and not let the price fall back to the initial entry point. Effectively it seeks to "lock in" profits as they increase.

Having placed so much stress on the role of a profit maximizing strategy, I want to show you in subsequent chapters various methods of maximizing day trade profits.

HOW THE VALUE OF STF MODEL CORRECTS OR ELIMINATES FAULTY TRADING BEHAVIORS

The STF model has distinct advantages over a disorganized or unstructured approach. Not only does it require a specific set of rules and procedures, but it also imposes a logical sequential approach on the decision-making and trade implementation process. In so doing, it corrects and eliminates faulty trading behaviors through adding structure and by helping to determine also facilitates the process of determining where, when, or how a trader erred.

Given that many market losses are a function of the trader and not the system, the STF structure allows you to readily identify and—hopefully—not repeat procedural missteps. It permits a definitive response to the question, "Was it the system that was correct or was it the trader who was incorrect?"

Systems are not perfect. They take losses, and such losses are acceptable. Traders, however, must strive for perfection in following the dictates of a system.

Although the methods and procedures of market entry I discuss in this book are reasonably objective and mechanical, the methods of market exit are not. Market exit methods will be more difficult to learn because a large part of it is subjective. STF helps to setup your exit with profitability targets, trailing stops and so forth, but it does leave some room for judgment.

INTERMEDIATE AND LONG-TERM TRADING WITH THE STF

The STF model is also applicable to trading in longer time frames. The rules of application in such cases are similar to those discussed for day trading except, of course, that trades need not be closed out at the end of the day session. However, I will not discuss these sorts of applications in this book.

MORE ABOUT FOLLOW-THROUGH

The day trader must exit his or her position by the end of the trading day. This, in turn, can undermine the use of a mechanical exit strategy. The day trader must strike while the iron is hot, taking profits when the opportunity presents itself. The decision as to when profits should be taken is often more of a procedural matter with relatively loose rules.

Those who advocate rigid adherence to a totally mechanical strategy for day trading will take issue with my point of view. Nonetheless my experience backs up my opinion. Accordingly, the exit strategies I will give you for each method are not mechanical or rigid. You will need to use some degree of judgment. This means that your results may well be different than the results of another trader. Clearly the role of experience comes into play when exiting day trade positions.

SUMMARY

Setup, Trigger, Follow-Through represents a basic approach to day trading that will save you from a lot of errors and problems. It is largely objective and mechanical, though there is some flexibility on the issue of when to exit, a point I'll take up in greater detail in future chapters. The most important point about the STF method is that it compels you, the trader, to follow a logical sequence of steps rather than reacting at random to fluctuations in the market.

Part 2 of this book explores specific trading methods and strategies that can be used within the STF framework.

SUCCESSFUL
METHODS OF
DAY TRADING

Chapter **5**

Gap Day Trading

Among the many methods that are compatible with
the Setup, Trigger, Follow-Through structure, we'll
start with so-called "gap trading." It is relatively simple
and not imbued with statistical analysis. As a trading
method, it also happens to be quite effective.

To understand gaps, we need to keep in the front of our minds that *the underlying engine of virtually all day trades is emotion.* The vast majority of intra-day market moves occur as a function of news. Whether the news is anticipated or not, it often results in a response by market participants. The response is motivated by how traders perceive the news. Perceptions invariably differ from one trader to another. When perceptions differ, so do actions. What may be considered positive news by one trader might be viewed negatively by another. What some traders will see as a buying opportunity others see as a reason to sell or go short. When news affects a particular market, that market tends to open on a gap.

A gap is simply a substantial difference between the opening price for a particular security at the start of a trading day and the high or low price from the previous day. If Intel has a high of $15 one day and opens at $16.10 the next, that's a significant "gap up" opening from the previous day. ("Gap up" because the opening price the following day is higher; if it were lower, we'd refer to it as a "gap down.")

When a gap occurs, it can either be news driven or driven by a real—or perceived—deluge of built up demand for, or supply of, the security. Gaps are often an emotional response or over-response to political news, announced corporate earnings, or other events. Gaps can build on themselves if market players sense some fundamental imbalance between supply and demand. Traders often use gaps to identify markets that are either excessively weak or strong.

TYPES OF GAPS AND WHY THEY WORK

As indicated at the start of this chapter, there are two types of gaps:

1. Opening Gap Up: When a market opens above the high of the previous day an up gap opening has occurred.
2. Opening Gap Down: When a market opens below the low of the previous day a down gap opening has occurred.

Within the STF framework, gap-up openings are setups to go short (i.e., sell with the intention of buying later at a lower price) while gap-down openings are usually setups to go long (i.e., buy with an intention of selling later at a higher price). Why? Because market makers and professional traders trade into gaps for their own profit.

When there's a big gap-up opening, the day traders' instinct is to sell short to the buyers knocking on the door, then cover that position later once the demand slackens. The effect of the large short sales pushes the market price of the stock down, and the price retreats below the previous high price.

For example, let's go back to the case of Intel, which had a high of $15 and opened the following day at $16.10. Intel market makers may well start to sell Intel stocks at the higher price of $16.10 in hopes to recover their share inventory (or cover their shorts, more likely the case with other professional traders) later on. Such a typical gap-up pattern is a setup for you to sell into the market. Extensive sales at the higher price will probably force the stock or security lower. (Many traders will recognize gap trades from the extensive work and expertise of Larry Williams who referred to gap trades as Oops Trades.)

Figure 5.1 illustrates a gap-up opening.

Gap Higher Opening

Figure 5.1 shows a gap higher opening. As you can see the opening price on the right is higher than the daily price bar high on the left.

GAP SET-UPS

As there are two types of gaps, so are there also two types of gap setups. The setup occurs when the price opens above or below the high or low from the previous day:

1. Buy Set-Up: A gap buy setup occurs when the opening price today is lower than the low price yesterday.
2. Sell Set-Up: A gap sell setup occurs when the opening price today is higher than the high price yesterday.

We saw this above with the Intel example. This was a gap sell setup, and we sold below the high of the previous day.

Gaps occur in both stocks and futures. Before looking at gap triggers, here are a few additional points about gaps of which you should be aware:

*   Gaps are not necessarily related to underlying trends in the market.

- Gap downs don't occur only when the market is in retreat. Some of the most profitable gap down openings have developed in underlying bull markets.
- Conversely, some of the most profitable gap up openings have developed in underlying bear markets.
- Gap days (i.e., days on which a given stock or commodity market opens either below the low of the previous day or above the high of the previous day) tend to produce large trading ranges.
- Gap days tend to be pivotal. By this I mean that many important tops and bottoms in stocks and futures occur on gap days.
- Gap days can often be high trading volume days.
- Twenty-four-hour trading has not eliminated gaps in futures markets. There are fewer gaps but they appear to be more reliable.

GAP TRIGGERS

The gap Set-Up occurs when the stock price opens above or below the price of the previous day. This confirmation of the gap pattern signals that the conditions are right for a trade. So, you can set a gap sell Trigger when the market price opens above the high of the previous day and then falls below the high of the previous day. When this occurs, it initiates a short position.

A gap buy Trigger occurs when the price, after an opening drop, rises above the low of the previous day; that triggers a buy for the stock. These gaps are said to be "filled" when a market falls back into the previous daily trading range after opening above it or vice versa.

Now let's look at the trigger for a gap lower opening. Figure 5.2 shows a gap lower opening. When the stock price trades back above the low of the previous bar, the gap is filled. A sell set up occurs when a gap higher opening develops. Under the impact of traders' selling, prices penetrate back down through the high of the previous day.

FOLLOW-THROUGHS FOR GAP TRADES

Figure 5.2. Gap lower open setup with a buy trigger.

Several types of Follow-Throughs for gap trades are possible. The simplest method involves a stop loss and exit at the end of the day. This approach can be used mechanically and does not require you to actively watch the market. Figure 5.3 shows the basic and most simple exit method for a gap buy trade.

Figure 5.3. Gap buy trade triggered and closed at the end of the day.

FIRST PROFITABLE OPENING FOLLOW-THROUGH

Another method for exit is to hold the trade overnight and to exit on the first profitable opening (FPO). An FPO is simply an opening that is profitable based on your entry price. Any profitable opening is acceptable as an exit strategy for this approach. The good news about using FPO exit is that it tends to increase the accuracy of the gap trade since it forces exit at a profit. It also tends to increase profitability. The bad news is that the transaction is no longer a day trade and thus becomes vulnerable to the impact of overnight news and other changes in market course. Although FPO falls outside the framework of day trading, I mention this exit strategy for those who want to have an alternate exit method.

Note that it is also possible to use a multiple exit strategy by trading, or splitting, multiple positions. If, for example you entered 400 shares on a gap trade buy you would exit all shares if the trade is not profitable at the end of the day (EOD). On the other hand, if the trade is profitable you could exit half the position at the end of the day and keep the remainder of the position for an FPO exit.

As an example of this exit strategy see Figure 5.4.

Figure 5.4. Gap buy trade closed out on FPO.

In the above example, we showed you how to enter on a gap buy trade. Alternately, you could enter on a gap sell trade, which works as the exact opposite of the gap buy trade.

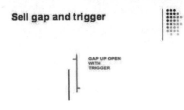

Figure 5.5. A sell gap and a trigger.

FINE TUNING THE TRADE

There are several additional variables that can be used as fine-tuning mechanisms for gap trades. Fine tuning increases the probability of success and prioritizes certain trade patterns and setups over others.

One of these variables is the *size* of the opening gap. For instance, a market can open a small amount or a large amount below the low of the previous day. As a general rule the larger the opening gap, the more likely you are to see a large move of the stock price, and the higher the ultimate probability of success of your trade. Note, however, that because large open-

Figure 5.6 illustrates the gap size concept.

ing gaps are less frequent than smaller ones, there will be fewer trades with large opening gaps; your option to employ this setup occurs less frequently.

Consistent with the idea that the gap trade is fairly simple and straightforward, there are a limited number of other fine-tuning variables for gap trades. One is the size of the gap compared to underlying volatility of the security; another is the speed at which the gap is filled. All of these variables are somewhat subjective and are likely influenced by your experience with the security, although some traders look for gap patterns across the board and may trade a security on a gap that they've never traded before.

GAP TRADE EXAMPLES

Gap patterns are fairly obvious and many occur frequently with certain securities. Let's look at some charts of actual buy and sell gap signals. The following four charts (Figures 5.7–5.10) illustrate buy and sell gap signals for a handful of securities: stocks of Xerox Corporation, Starbucks, Dell Computer, and Archer-Daniels-Midland and the S&P 500 E-Mini futures contract. As you review these charts you'll learn to recognize the setups and triggers. Note also the reality of the fact that not every setup has a trigger; that is, not every gap retraces, thus no trigger is "pulled," thus no trade is signaled.

Note again in Figure 5.8 that an opening gap does not become a triggered trade unless it penetrates the previous daily low or high. In the case of SBUX, several gaps were not filled and did not, therefore, trigger.

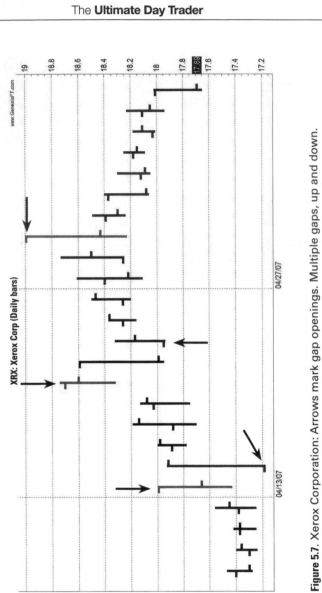

Figure 5.7. Xerox Corporation: Arrows mark gap openings. Multiple gaps, up and down.

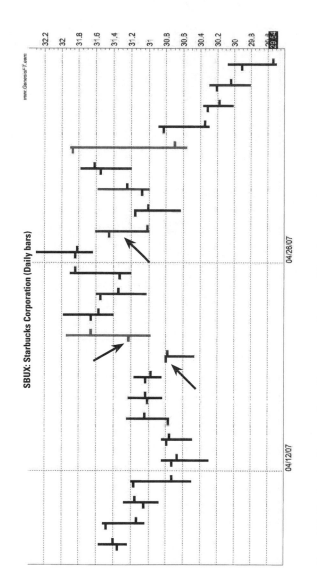

Figure 5.8. Starbucks Corporation: Gaps set up but not filled (triggered) shown by arrows.

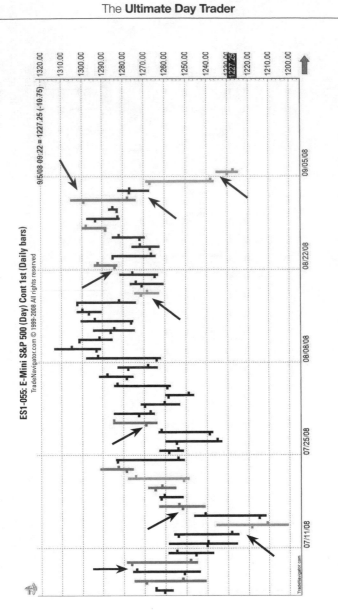

Figure 5.9. E-Mini S&P 500 mixed bag: triggers, non-triggers, losing trades (see arrows).

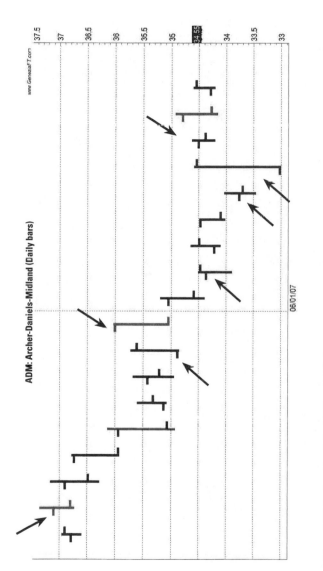

Figure 5.10 Archer-Daniels-Midland: Of the seven gap trades shown on this chart five were profitable. You will observe that the largest-range trading day on this chart is a gap day. Gap days tend to have large trading ranges, which are a reflection of their highly emotional component (see arrows).

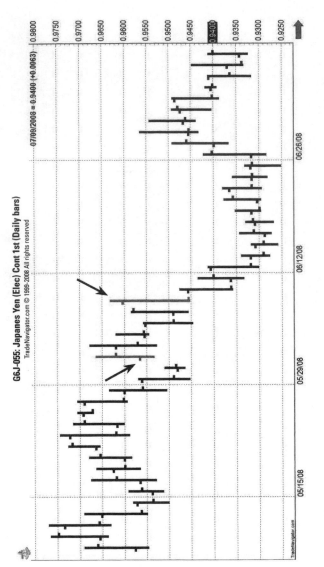

Figure 5.11. Japanese Yen futures: There were only two gap days on this chart. One gap was not filled and one did not trigger. The gap that was filled was very profitable. You will also note that the gap that was triggered was a large range day. As I have pointed out earlier, gap days tend to have large ranges due to their emotional aspect (see arrows).

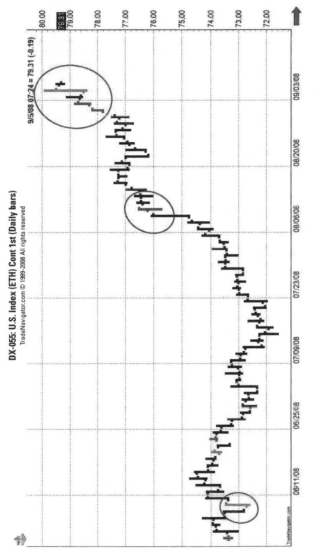

Figure 5.12. U.S. Dollar Index: This chart shows a number of gap trades in the U.S. dollar index futures. Clearly not all of the gaps were profitable. Remember that I am not suggesting that the gap method is 100 percent accurate. I am, however, suggesting that in the long run your day trading gap profits will be larger in sum total than your gap day trading losses, provided you follow the rules and provided you use a profit maximizing strategy.

Of the fourteen gaps shown in Figure 5.9, five were profitable, six failed to trigger, and the rest were losing trades. By the Follow-Through rules I have noted in the test, the sum total of the profitable trades was larger than the sum total of the losing trades.

GAPS IN FUTURES MARKETS: FEWER BUT BETTER

Since the start of twenty-three-hour trading in the currency futures markets, there have been fewer gaps in these markets. The fact that there is only a one-hour hiatus from the close of one session to the opening of the next session (except on weekends) gives the markets little time to react to news that might cause an opening gap. Hence, there are fewer gaps. I have found, nonetheless, that in spite of the lower frequency of gaps, those that do develop tend to be more profitable. Here are some examples.

There were only two gap days on this chart. One gap was not filled and one did not trigger. The gap that filled was very profitable.

FINE TUNING THE FOLLOW-THROUGH

Like Set-Ups and Triggers, there are many ways to fine-tune the exit strategies for gap trades. Here are a few:

- Exit at stop loss.
- Exit at profit target.

- Exit on first profitable opening.
- Combined strategy on multiple contacts.
  - Exit one at profit target 1 and raise stop to break even.
  - Exit one at end of day.
  - Exit one on FPO.

STOP LOSS EXIT

I have given you several strategies to exit at a profit. Now let's look at the stop loss exit. There are several types of stop losses that can be used in this or any day trade. The simple dollar profit risk stop is not acceptable to me because it is artificial. It is usually based on how much a trader is willing to lose or able to lose on a trade. The market has no respect for such stops. They are not logical. Stops should be based on market behavior such as indicators, volatility, price ranges, and so on.

Here are some additional gap trade examples. Remember to consider the variables:

- Size of gap in cents or ticks—the bigger the gap the better the trade
- Amount of penetration into previous daily low (in cents or ticks)
- Size of stop loss
- Initial profit target

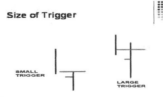

Figure 5.13. Size of trigger.

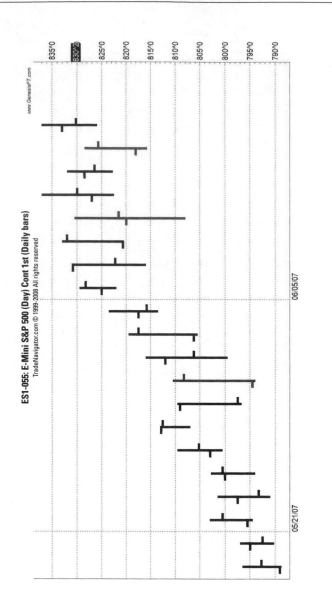

Figure 5.14. Actual gap buys, soybean futures. In Figure 5.15 there are eight gap trades (marked by arrows). Of these, five reached their profit targets.

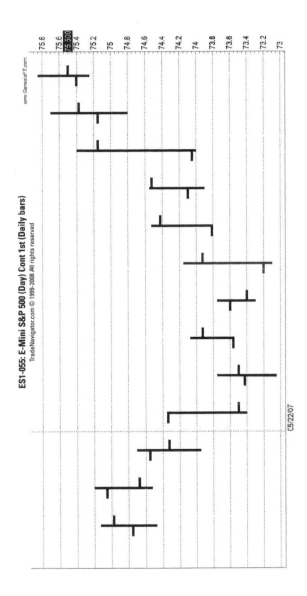

Figure 5.15. A gap buy and exit: lean hogs.

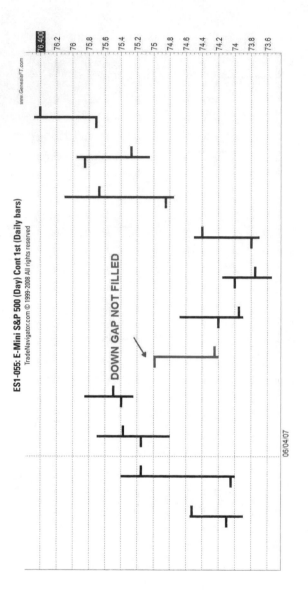

Figure 5.16. Gap down not filled (no trade).

In the case of Figure 5.15 the market opened gap lower and then triggered a buy. It reached its profit target and closed the day well above its previous close. The next opening was a profitable opening, but it was not the best profit that could have been achieved. I draw your attention to the fact that after the gap trade ended, the market continued to move considerable higher. In this case as in many others, a trailing stop profit-maximizing strategy would have worked extremely well to lock in a much larger profit.

There were two gaps on the chart shown in Figure 5.16 that were not filled. A gap that is not filled does not trigger a trade. The rule is simple: no trigger, no trade. Do not anticipate a trigger on any of the methods that I show you in this book.

GAP TRADING TRACK RECORDS

To illustrate the advantages of gap trading, here is an "all trades report" showing gap trading profits:

GAP TRADE S&P PERCENTAGE PROFIT

Target Exit

Overall			
Total Net Profit	$147,100	Profit Factor ($Wins/$Losses)	1.3
Total Trades	379	Winning Percentage	74.9%
Average Trade	$388	Payout Ratio (Avg Win/Loss)	10.45

Overall (con't)			
Avg # of Bars in Trade	1.55	Z-Score (W/L Predictability)	−0.8
Avg # of Trades per Year	42.3	Percent in the Market	24.9%
Max Closed-out Drawdown	−$75,075	Max Intra-day Drawdown	−$75,075
Account Size Required	$92,393	Return Pct	159.2%
Open Equity	$0	Kelly Ratio	0.1868
Current Streak	1 Win	Optimal f	0.30
Winning Trades		**Losing Trades**	
Total Winners	284	Total Losers	95
Gross Profit	$590,000	Gross Loss	−$442,900
Average Win	$2,077	Average Loss	−$4,662
Largest Win	$7,325	Largest Loss	−$9,200
Largest Drawdown in Win	−$4,675	Largest Peak in Loss	$3,850
Avg Drawdown in Win	−$566	Avg Peak in Loss	$1,176
Avg Run Up in Win	$2,099	Avg Run Up in Loss	$1,176
Avg Run Down in Win	−$566	Avg Run Down in Loss	−$4,962

Most Consec Wins	33	Most Consec Losses	5
Avg # of Consec Wins	4.12	Avg # of Consec Losses	1.40
Avg # of Bars in Wins	1.12	Avg # of Bars in Losses	2.84

Figure 5.17 Summary of S&P gap trades with exit at percentage profit target. By waiting for a profit target exit you increase the percentage accuracy as well as the profits. By exiting at the end of the day the percentage odds are lower, as is the average profit per trade.

CHARACTERISTICS OF GAP TRADES

Let me sum up some general points about gap trades. Over time and with experience, I've found the following to be true about gaps and gap trades:

- Gaps are not necessarily related to underlying trends.
- Some of the most profitable gap-down openings have developed in underlying bull markets.
- Some of the most profitable gap-up openings have developed in underlying bear markets.
- Gap days tend to produce large trading ranges.
- Gap days tend to be pivotal. Many important tops and bottoms occur on gap days in stocks and futures.
- Gap days can often be high trading volume days.
- Twenty-four-hour trading has not eliminated gaps in futures markets. There are fewer gaps but they appear to be more reliable.
- Gaps work for stocks as well as futures.

Bearing these points in mind, consider including gap trades among your arsenal of day-trading strategies.

Chapter **6**

The Moving Average Channel with Confirmation Trend and Channel Trading

Some day traders attempt to profit from the "spread";
that is, they trade based on the difference between bid
and offer price. This generally affords relatively small
gains. For years, traders in search of larger profits have
gravitated toward identifying trends and trading ranges
around those trends. In fact, two of the most well-
known and widely used methods for trading stocks and
commodities are support-and-resistance trading and
trend trading.

The techniques used in these methods range from the relatively simple visual observance of chart patterns to highly sophisticated quantitative measurement of trends, trend reversals, and trading ranges around trends.

In this chapter, I'll cover simple trend trading, support-and resistance trading, and my version of the Moving Average Channel (MAC) method. The MAC method, with a confirming indicator, can be used for day trading with the underlying trend and/or for support-and-resistance trading in the direction of the existing trend. For each method, I'll outline the Set-Up, Trigger and Follow-Through stages.

The key to effectively using trends in day trading is to know the current trend and understand how to spot trend changes. When combined with a quantifiable approach for determining support and resistance, trend-based trading offers excellent potential for profits.

SUPPORT AND RESISTANCE

Markets, and securities within markets, don't go straight up or down. They usually go up or down within a trading range around a trend line, whether that trend line is up, down, or sideways. Support and resistance trading captures movements around that trend line.

The theory or concept of support and resistance trading is simple: If a market is moving higher then, at least theoretically, there should be a price level at which buyers are willing to "support" prices on declines within the existing upward trend. In a declining market there should be a price level at which sellers are willing to sell short within the existing downward trend.

Support and resistance trading is among the most widely used of trading methods. The traditional approach to support and resistance trading has been to draw up and down trend lines on a chart. Virtually every introductory course on technical analysis teaches this approach. In order to determine trend changes, most methods chart moving averages based on closing prices. Those traders preparing and following the charts use traditional support and resistance lines (i.e., trend lines) to determine buy and/or sell points within the existing trend.

DEFINING SUPPORT AND RESISTANCE

Figure 6.1 shows the typical support and resistance method. The good news about this approach is that it is simple. The bad news is that it is subjective. The method of application is simple. When prices decline to support in an up trend, a "long," or a buy, is established. When prices rally to resistance in a down trend a short is established. As you can see from the chart, the placement of a trend line is critically important. Where you place the line and how much variance you allow in the touch or penetration of a line can make the difference between a profit or a loss.

SHORTCOMINGS OF TRADITIONAL SUPPORT-AND-RESISTANCE METHODS

On Figure 6.1, I have drawn both an up trend and a down trend line. I have circled areas of sell and buy points. While the approach may look good "on paper," it is not sufficiently objective when examined in detail. For example, how much of a penetration of the trend line is acceptable? What constitutes a change in trend? How do we define the risks? When do we take profits?

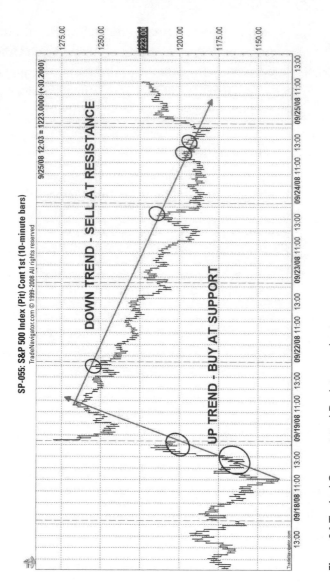

Figure 6.1 Typical Support and Resistance chart.

As you can see, there are some issues with regard to the traditional support and resistance trend line methods. In a perfect world with 20/20 hindsight, trend line trading appears to be a winning approach. But is it valid? Is it objective? Does it get results? The only certain answer is to subject the method to a hard statistical test but there are clearly some issues in doing so. Among these are the following:

- How do you define a trend line objectively?
- How to do you determine what constitutes a successful trade?
- Is there a purely objective way of determining when and if trend line support or resistance are hit?

While the trend line method is intuitive and simple, it's easy to get fooled by trend changes and in particular major trend reversals. It also doesn't lend itself to setting quantitative or objective trading rules, the STF framework included.

TRADITIONAL MOVING AVERAGE METHODS

Moving average (MA) methods attempt to smooth the random noise of the market into moving averages to give a clearer idea of true trends and ranges. Traditional moving average–based systems, while popular and widely used, are not known for their accuracy. Typically their reliability is well below 50 percent, and drawdowns are large. Traders who have large accounts can eventually fare well with such systems if they are financially and psychologically able to deal with the large number of consecutive losses as well as the large drawdowns.

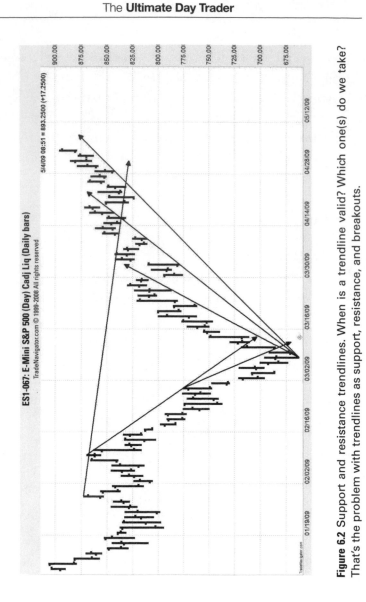

Figure 6.2 Support and resistance trendlines. When is a trendline valid? Which one(s) do we take? That's the problem with trendlines as support, resistance, and breakouts.

One of the more popular moving average based methods is the 200 period moving average. The concept and methodology are simple. When prices close below their 200 period—a

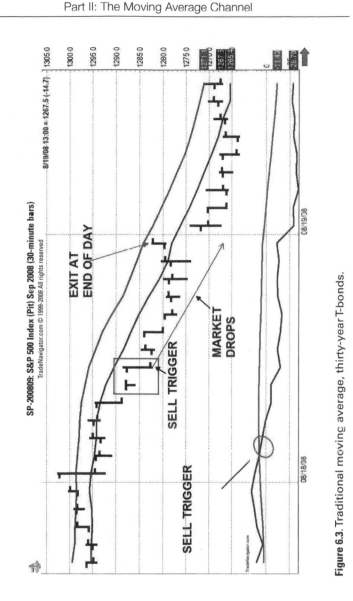

Figure 6.3. Traditional moving average, thirty-year T-bonds.

"crossover" MA—a sell signal is triggered. When prices close above their 200 day MA, a sell is triggered. While the method is widely followed and often cited on major business radio and television shows as well as by trading advisers, the statistics tell a very different story.

It is a known fact among traders that traditional MA methods are effective trend following systems but that they tend to perform very poorly in non-trending markets and/or when markets change direction. Traditional MA based systems tend to give back a considerable amount of profit when trends change. Note that by "traditional" I mean MA systems that buy or sell on closing MA crossover signals. Figures 6.2 and 6.3 illustrate such signals on a daily chart of T-bond futures.

Note that in Figure 6.2 the signals aren't particularly clear or telling when the trend is unclear. Also note how the signal at the top lags the sharpest moves.

TRADING WITH THE MOVING AVERAGE CHANNEL

The moving average channel method (MAC) is a method I developed and introduced over twenty years ago. It has become a standard for many traders who use support and resistance concepts in their work. The methodology is simple.

The MAC uses two moving averages, one of the high for each price bar and one of the low. The input values of the moving averages are ten and eight periods respectively. The moving average (MA) is a simple, linear, not an exponential average weighting more recent periods more heavily. I have found this combination to be most effective.

The two averages are used as support and resistance levels combined with an analysis of the trend. Figure 6.4 shows the application of my moving average channel method with a

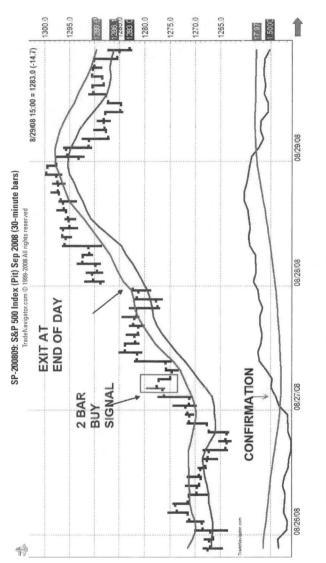

SP-200809: S&P 500 Index (Pit) Sep 2008 (30-minute bars)

8/29/08 15:00 = 1283.0 (-14.7)

EXIT AT
END OF DAY

2 BAR
BUY
SIGNAL

CONFIRMATION

Figure 6.4. MAC chart, declining market, S&P 500 Index (30 minute bars).

confirming signal in an up-trending market. The upper line shows a 10 period simple MA of high while the lower line shows a simple 8 period MA of lows.

In Figure 6.4, using the thirty minute S&P 500 futures chart, two consecutive price bars completely below the 8 MA of the lows mark the start of a down trend. The trend is confirmed with the use of the 28 period Momentum indicator and its 28 period simple moving average (shown at the bottom of the chart). When the Momentum indicator crosses its moving average, it gives a sell signal (the first "sell trigger" on the chart). When the channel boundary is exceeded and the confirmation signal is giving or has already given the same signal, the trade is triggered. After the sell signal, prices decline until thirty minutes prior to the end of the day. Exit at the end of the day and/ or on a profit target would have resulted in a profit.

Figure 6.5 shows my application of this method for day trading in a rising market:

The charts shown are intra-day charts, but the method can be used in any time frame. If the MAC is used in time frames other than intra-day, then the confirming trend indicator (MOM, or Momentum, and its MA) should be a different length. Some readers may be familiar with my MAC application on daily charts. In such cases I prefer to use a 57 period simple moving average of the MOM or Williams Accumulation/Distribution (AD) with its 57 period moving average.

For those who trade stocks as opposed to futures, the technique can be applied to the SPY (Spyder) which is the stock equivalent of S&P 500 futures.

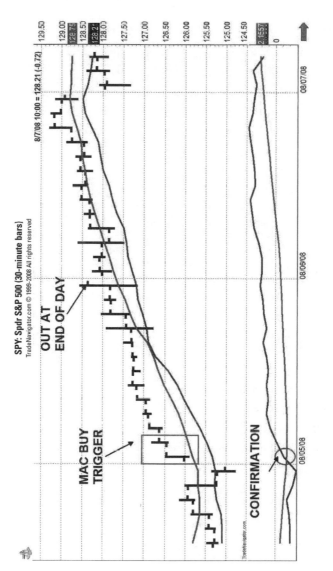

SPY: Spdr S&P 500 (30-minute bars)

OUT AT
END OF DAY

MAC BUY
TRIGGER

CONFIRMATION

8/7'08 10:00 = 128.21 (-0.72)

129.50
129.00
128.75
128.50
128.21
128.00
127.50
127.00
126.50
126.00
125.50
125.00
124.50
2.1557
0

08/05/08   08/06/08   08/07/08

Figure 6.5. S&P futures thirty-minute chart with MAC signals and confirmation.

MAC TRADING METHOD APPLIED

Here are the rules of application for day trading using the MAC trend signals along with a few more examples:

Determine the current market trend. This is done by looking at the number of consecutive price bars above or below the Moving Average Channel. Two complete consecutive price bars above the MA high line is considered a buy pattern. The confirmation signal at the bottom is a trigger. In Figure 6.5, the "2-Bar Buy Signal" gives the pattern, the MOM/MA crossover at the bottom confirms the signal. The consecutive complete price bars above the MA high constitutes a new bull trend when confirmed with MOM/MA in bullish mode.

- **Two complete consecutive price bars below the 8 period MA of the low constitutes a sell pattern** which, when confirmed by MOM/MA below its MA confirms a sell trigger.
- **Decide on Follow-Through**. The resulting trade can be closed out at support or resistance (i.e., the opposite signal) or it may be carried with a trailing stop to the end of the session. Alternatively it can be closed out at a predetermined resistance point.

USING THE MAC FOR SUPPORT AND RESISTANCE TRADING

The MAC method described above can also be used for support and resistance trading. By this I mean simply that you will buy at support and sell at resistance consistent with an established trend. The trend is determined by the same trigger(s) that are used for the MAC timing triggers noted above. Here are the procedures followed by a chart example. For many markets and securities, trends will reverse several times within a day, providing trading opportunities throughout. The MAC method will signal trades throughout. Note that, just as with the gap trades shown in Chapter 5, not all of these trades will be confirmed or "triggered" by the MOM/MA tracking indicator. Figure 6.6 shows multiple trend and channel changes through the trading day, all confirmed by the tracking indicator:

SUMMARY OF THE MAC WITH CONFIRMATION

In the end, support and resistance and Moving Average Channel methods are part of the core "toolbox" for the day trader. There are many more ways to construct these setups, particularly for the MAC, using different metrics. The best choice will depend on the security you're trading, your level of experience, and the success of that experience with the chosen method. Like most elements of day trading, success comes with clear understanding, practice, and hard work.

The MAC is a simple but powerful concept. While it uses moving averages, it does not do so in the traditional sense. Rather than use moving averages of closing prices (which is the traditional approach), the MAC uses moving averages of the high and the low. A buy set-up and a sell set-up must be confirmed with the Momentum moving average indicator as noted earlier. The MAC with confirmation can be used in any time frame in stocks, futures, or FOREX. As also noted previ-

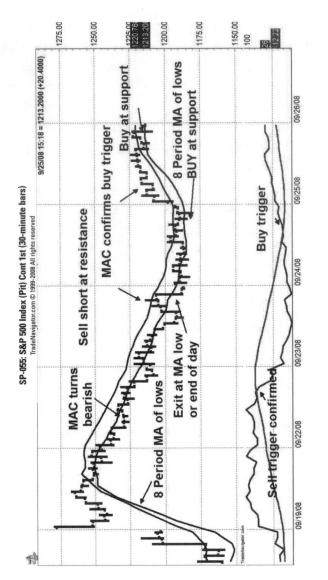

Figure 6.6. S&P 500 Index, thirty-minute bars.

ously, the use of a profit-maximizing strategy is essential. The MAC can be used as a trend change indicator as well as an indicator of support and resistance.

The next method, covered in Chapter 7, is the "day of week pattern," which is also totally objective but which is based on a concept that is foreign to many day traders.

Chapter **7**

Day Trading by the Day

What is a "Day of Week Pattern"? Many traders believe

that the stock and commodity markets have reliable

and predictable patterns based on the day of the week.

Yale Hirsch in his excellent 1986 book, *Don't Sell Stocks*

on Monday (now out of print), discussed the tendency

for stocks to bottom on Mondays. He provided a

lengthy historical validation for his claim. This raises a

number of questions:

- Is it possible that other days of the week are also predictable as up or down days?
- Are there other day-to-day relationships that could prove valuable to the day trader?
- Are these days consistent across markets or do certain markets display specific day-of-week characteristics?
- If so, then how can these patterns be incorporated into a day trading strategy?

I have performed a considerable amount of research on this topic and I have come to some significant conclusions. Before we continue, let's look at a few definitions:

- **Day of Week Pattern:** I use this term to define a pattern that occurs within the course of a day with regard to the opening and closing price. It also refers to the relationship between the closing price one day and the closing price the next day.
- **Open vs. Close Relationship**: This is the comparison of the opening price and the closing price on the same day.

STF DEFINITIONS FOR DAY OF WEEK PATTERN TRADING

In my work I have discovered a relationship between the behavior of S&P futures prices (as well as a number of other markets) on Monday (or the first trading day of the week) and Friday (or the last trading day of the week). Here are the Set-Up, Trigger, and Follow-Through details for this relationship:

- **Set-Up**: If the closing price on the last trading day of the week is *greater than* the opening price, then the Set-Up is for a *buy* on Monday or the first trading day of the week. If the closing price on the last trading day of the week is *less than* the opening price, then the Set-Up is for a *sell* on Monday or the first trading day of the week.

- **Trigger**: For a Monday buy Set-Up, the Trigger is a *buy stop* rise of a given number of points on Monday *above* the high of Friday. For a sell Trigger we use a *sell stop* price a given number of points *below* the low of Friday. Buy stops and sell stops are used at these points to enter these positions. Note that the number of points required to trigger varies from market to market but generally even a few ticks or cents (for stocks) will do. If this method seriously interests you, you can determine the best number of points by running an optimization program on that particular stock or commodity. (For those who are concerned about overly optimizing this or any methodology, I refer you to my discussion of optimization in Chapter 2.)

- **The Follow-Through** consists of a stop loss and exit at the end of the day. Traders who are willing and able to carry positions overnight can do so.

THE CASE FOR AND AGAINST DAY OF WEEK PATTERNS

There will be those who doubt the validity or existence of day of week patterns such as the one described in this chapter. To answer them, I'd like to share some statistics with you about the day of week method I have developed. Before I do so I'd like to establish a few important points about the day of week pattern. Note the following:

- The day of week pattern (DOW) is not a day trade *per se* since it requires holding a position until the next opening. I have included the DOW in this book because the "day trade" as we have come to know it has changed considerably with the advent of twenty-four-hour or near twenty-four-hour trading.
- In currency futures, for example, the market is open twenty-three hours a day. There is a one-hour hiatus from the close of trading on one day and the open of trading the next day.
- The holding period for a day trade is therefore considerably longer than it has ever been.
- The day trader can trade within the twenty-three-hour time frame or "break the rules" slightly and exit one hour later when the market opens again.

What you do is clearly a matter of personal preference and finances. Figure 7.1 shows an example of a DOW trade in the European currency futures.

STATISTICS DON'T LIE

While the concept may appear valid, the question critics ask is whether the method actually works. While I cannot guarantee the future performance of this approach, I can show you some compelling statistics regarding its historical validity in various markets. Consider the examples that follow.

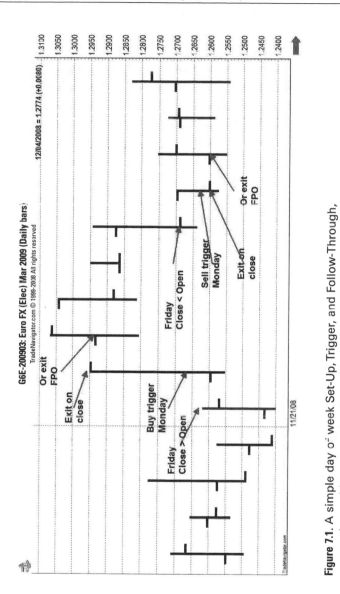

Figure 7.1. A simple day of week Set-Up, Trigger, and Follow-Through, one on the upside, one on the downside.

DOW EXAMPLES

Here are two examples of the DOW method in a stock and in a futures market. Let's look at the DOW relationship in Google (NASDAQ: GOOG). Note the trigger values and the stop loss values as described.

SUMMARY—ALL TRADES

Overall			
Total Net Profit	$74,661	Profit Factor ($Wins/$Losses)	1.50
Total Trades	140	Winning Percentage	75.0%
Average Trade	$533	Payout Ratio (Avg Win/Loss)	0.50
Avg # of Bars in Trade	1.46	Z-Score (W/L Predictability)	0.2
Avg # of Trades per Year	32.0	Percent in the Market	18.5%
Max Closed-out Drawdown	**–$17,901**	Max Intraday Drawdown	**–$20,916**
Account Size Required	$20,916	Return Pct	357.0%
Open Equity	$1,773	Kelly Ratio	0.2513
Current Streak	1 Losses	Optimal f	0.41

Winning Trades		Losing Trades	
Total Winners	105	Total Losers	35
Gross Profit	$222,795	Gross Loss	**−$148,134**
Average Win	$2,122	Average Loss	**−$4,232**
Largest Win	$11,865	Largest Loss	**−$8,664**
Largest Drawdown in Win	**−$4,641**	Largest Peak in Loss	$4,764
Avg Drawdown in Win	**−$856**	Avg Peak in Loss	$815
Avg Run Up in Win	$2,853	Avg Run Up in Loss	$815
Avg Run Down in Win	**−$856**	Avg Run Down in Loss	**−$4,269**
Most Consec Wins	10	Most Consec Losses	3
Avg # of Consec Wins	3.89	Avg # of Consec Losses	1.30
Avg # of Bars in Wins	1.43	Avg # of Bars in Losses	1.54

Figure 7.2. Day of week trade, Friday-Monday in GOOG using 300 shares with exit on first profitable opening and the following entry and stop loss points. Long positions buy stop 32 cents above the Friday high with stop loss of $4,700. Short positions sell stop 40 cents below Friday low with $3,800 stop loss. Note the significant Profit Factor of 1.5 as well as a 75 percent winning percentage and a payout ratio of .50. In addition, the method yielded a strong return percentage of 357 percent. Negative statistics are in boldface.

Here is another example of the DOW approach, this one in Potash (POT), another active stock that is appropriate for this method.

SUMMARY—ALL TRADES

Overall			
Total Net Profit	$27,318	Profit Factor ($Wins/$Losses)	1.89
Total Trades	77	Winning Percentage	83.1%
Average Trade	$355	Payout Ratio (Avg Win/Loss)	0.38
Avg # of Bars in Trade	2.35	Z-Score (W/L Predictability)	**−2.1**
Avg # of Trades per Year	17.9	Percent in the Market	12.9%
Max Closed-out Drawdown	**−$8,100**	Max Intraday Drawdown	**−$8,115**
Account Size Required	$8,115	Return Pct	336.6%
Open Equity	$1,242	Kelly Ratio	0.3906
Current Streak	8 Wins	Optimal f	0.38
Winning Trades		**Losing Trades**	
Total Winners	64	Total Losers	13
Gross Profit	$58,134	Gross Loss	**−$30,816**

Winning Trades (con't)		Losing Trades (con't)	
Average Win	$908	Average Loss	**−$2,370**
Largest Win	$6,342	Largest Loss	**−$2,811**
Largest Drawdown in Win	**−$2,694**	Largest Peak in Loss	$1,287
Avg Drawdown in Win	**−$535**	Avg Peak in Loss	$358
Avg Run Up in Win	$1,214	Avg Run Up in Loss	$358
Avg Run Down in Win	**−$535**	Avg Run Down in Loss	**−$2,370**
Most Consec Wins	17	Most Consec Losses	3
Ave # of Consec Wins	7.11	Avg # of Consec Losses	1.63
Avg # of Bars in Wins	2.02	Avg # of Bars in Losses	4.00

Figure 7.3. POTASH (POT) DOW report using the Friday–Monday relationship. Buy trade triggers at Friday high plus 48 cents with a $2,700 stop loss and sell trades trigger at Friday low minus 48 cents with a $2,200 stop loss. Data are for 300 shares per trade with exit on FPO. Again, note a significant profit factor of 1.89 and a winning percentage of 83.1. Negatives in the chart are given in boldface.

Looking at the percentage accuracy of the DOW over the course of many trades, it is reasonable to expect high accuracy. The extent of the profits will depend more on your skills as a trader than on the back-tested historical performance of the DOW method.

The big money is made in the big move. The longer you can ride a profitable trade with a trailing stop, the greater will be your profits. This is simple and totally objective with regard to market entry. The key is to back test the markets you want to trade and to follow the suggestions given above.

OTHER DAY OF WEEK RELATIONSHIPS

Based on my research there are other day of week relationships that show reasonably high accuracy. These should be investigated for possible implementation. As an example, consider the follow performance history in GOOG based on the Wednesday–Thursday relationship.

SUMMARY—ALL TRADES

Overall			
Total Net Profit	$53,916	Profit Factor ($Wins/$Losses)	1.29
Total Trades	136	Winning Percentage	68.4%
Average Trade	$396	Payout Ratio (Avg Win/Loss)	0.60
Avg # of Bars in Trade	1.61	Z-Score (W/L Predictability)	**–0.7**
Avg # of Trades per Year	31.3	Percent in the Market	19.9%
Max Closed-out Drawdown	**–$35,694**	Max Intraday Drawdown	**–$35,694**
Account Size Required	$35,694	Return Pct	151.1%

Overall (con't)			
Open Equity	$0	Kelly Ratio	0.1550
Current Streak	3 Wins	Optimal f	0.26
Winning Trades		**Losing Trades**	
Total Winners	93	Total Losers	43
Gross Profit	$237,831	Gross Loss	**−$183,915**
Average Win	$2,557	Average Loss	$4,277
Largest Win	$22,944	Largest Loss	$11,580
Largest Drawdown in Win	**−$4602**	Largest Peak in Loss	$3,468
Avg Drawdown in Win	**−$1,037**	Avg Peak in Loss	$630
Avg Run Up in Win	$3,065	Avg Run Up in Loss	$630
Avg Run Down in Win	**−$1,037**	Avg Run Down in Loss	**−$4,277**
Most Consec Wins	10	Most Consec Losses	6
Avg # of Consec Wins	3.32	Avg # of Consec Losses	1.54
Avg # of Bars in Wins	1.69	Avg # of Bars in Losses	1.44

Figure 7.4. The Wednesday–Thursday DOW record in GOOG using 45 cents as the buy and sell trigger with $4,800 stop loss on longs and $3,400 stops on shorts and FPO exit. Note the strong winning percentage of 68.4. All negative numbers in the chart are given in boldface.

MAXIMIZING DAY OF WEEK PROFITS RELATIONSHIPS IN OTHER MARKETS

The odds are that day-of-week relationships exist in all markets, stocks, and futures. Given that the strategy calls for exit either at the end of the day or on the first profitable opening, the profit potential in exploiting these relationships is limited. Since profits may be relatively small due to the brief holding period, the serious day trader must compensate for small moves with either of several profit maximizing strategies. They are as follows:

- **Trade with higher leverage using stock or futures options**. If you follow this strategy then you will need to use high delta options, that is, options that will move closely with the underlying stock or futures contract. You will also need to use limit orders so as to capture as much profit as possible by avoiding poor price executions.
- **Trade larger positions** (i.e., a larger number of shares or contracts) in order to increase bottom line profits.
- **Carry at least part of your winning positions over to the next day** or days using a trailing stop procedure and, in so doing, lock in more profit in the event that your trades continue to move in your favor.

CONVERTING THE DAY OF WEEK PATTERN TO A TRADING METHODOLOGY

While the DOW is a valid concept, the practical issue is how it translates into day trading profits. Here are some suggestions and directions regarding the implementation of the DOW methodology:

1. Determine the markets in which you want to use the DOW. Active stocks and commodity markets are better performers. By "active" I mean at least 5 million shares on average daily or at least 10,000 futures contracts on average daily.
2. Check the historical performance record of the markets you have selected. You can do this either manually or by using one of the available charting programs that have back testing capability.
3. Track the trades for a few weeks in real time to see if the relationship is stable and if potential profits are being generated.
4. Wait until the method has had two or three consecutive losing trades before you implement it. While this will take patience I believe it will increase your odds of getting started in a profitable direction.

Chapter **8**

Volume Spikes and Their Use in Day Trading

Volume in the stock and futures markets is a measure of market activity. Market activity, in turn, is a reflection of trader interest. Trader interest varies according to underlying fundamentals and/or technical developments. Whereas the traditional view is that fundamentals ultimately determine prices, I do not necessarily believe that all-encompassing statement. From time to time prices and fundamentals are out of phase with each other.

When traders and investors panic based on their perceptions of underlying fundamentals, they tend to over-react. Whether they do so as buyers or as sellers, their over-reaction is revealed in trading activity or volume. We can, therefore, use volume, both on a daily and intra-day basis, to help us make trading decisions.

VOLUME: WHAT IT IS, WHAT IT MEANS

Volume in stocks is the term used to express the number of shares traded during a given time frame (i.e., hourly, daily, or weekly). Volume in futures is measured by the number of contracts traded. Figures 8.1 and 8.2 show trading volume on a stock and futures chart respectively using intra-day data.

For many years trading volume data was not available during the day. With the advent of electronic trading and order entry, traders can now have up-to-the-minute volume information, which can be of significant value in making trading decisions. It is now possible to make those decisions based on exaggerated trading volume changes, known as volume spikes. Let's look more closely at "volume spikes."

WHAT IS A VOLUME SPIKE?

The precise definition of "volume spike" (VS) varies according to the technical trader and his or her orientation. Generally, however, spike in volume is defined as a large increase in volume from one time frame to another. I believe that a VS is a measure of trader emotion. If we accept the theory that

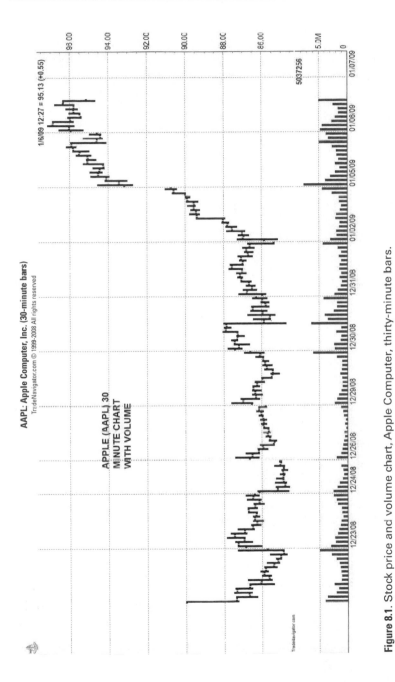

Figure 8.1. Stock price and volume chart, Apple Computer, thirty-minute bars.

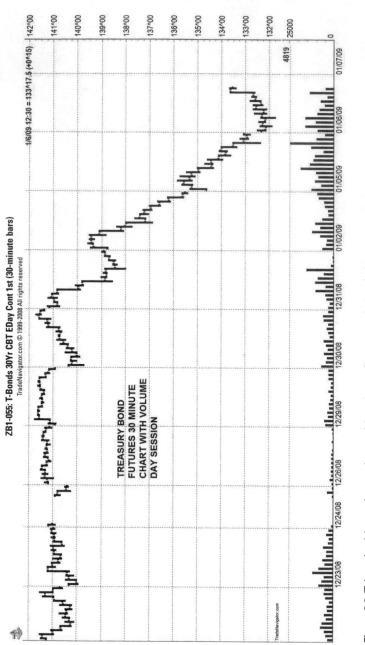

Figure 8.2. T bonds thirty-minute chart with volume (bottom of chart). Note especially the volume bars at the bottom of the chart. The larger the bar, the higher the volume.

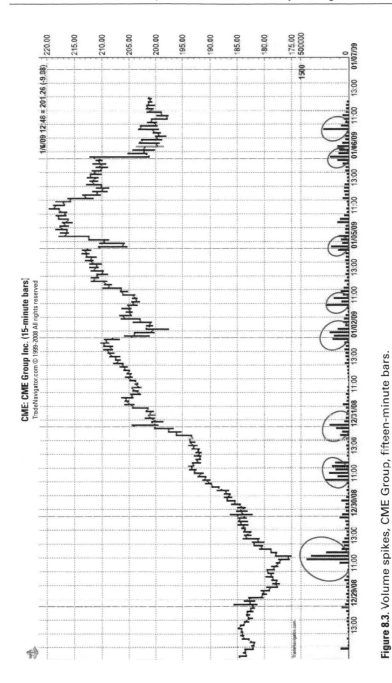

Figure 8.3. Volume spikes, CME Group, fifteen-minute bars.

extreme panic selling leads to bottoms and extreme panic buying leads to tops, we should consider only large increases in volume, representing as they do strong swings in trader emotions. I consider a fourfold increase in volume as a valid VS. In other words, if trading volume in a stock today is 1 million shares then, based on my definition, an increase to 8 million shares or more would be considered a VS. Consider figures 8.3–8.4 showing volume spikes:

The volume information runs along the bottom of the chart. Note the eight circled volume spikes.

On the chart for trading in the E-Mini S&P500 (Figure 8.4), note again the two circled volume spikes. Although the volume during the early minutes of 1/6/2009 is almost as high as the "spike" volume, it isn't a spike because volume had been generally increasing before that point in time.

OPERATIONAL DEFINITION OF A VOLUME SPIKE

How we choose to define a VS is integral to the success of any day trading method that depends on volume. For our purposes we will define a VS as an increase of at least fourfold in volume over a period of a maximum of at least four price bars. A review of the last two figures will give you a good idea of what the spikes look like. These parameters could easily be entered into a software charting program to help automate the search process. I will discuss more about this aspect of trade selection later.

I should note that typically stocks and commodities tend to have volume spikes when they first open for the day and when they close. We shouldn't entirely discount these volume

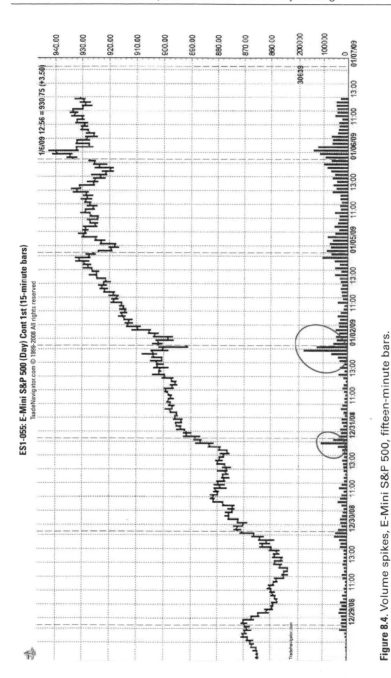

Figure 8.4. Volume spikes, E-Mini S&P 500, fifteen-minute bars.

movements, but I stress again that we are not interested simply in spikes but in spikes that are in the area of about fourfold the previous volume amounts. So we should be cautious about basing our trades on opening and closing volume spikes, especially if they are less than fourfold the previous volume.

TRADE TRIGGERS USING SPIKES

Given that spikes are caused by traders' highly emotional responses to news and/or fundamental data (e.g., the president makes a speech, there's a coup in Fiji, the government releases a report on housing starts), the odds are good that spikes often mark important turning points both on an intra-day and on a longer-term basis. This approach needs to be backed up by an operational procedure. Here is what I recommend.

1. Isolate a volume spike on an intra-day chart. I prefer the ten-minute chart for this purpose.
2. Note the price bar high and low for the period of the spike.
3. Buy on a bar **close** above the price high.
4. Sell on a bar **close** below the price low.
5. Use the opposite side of the trade for a stop loss.
6. Exit by the end of the session, or
7. Hold part of your position with a trailing stop if the trade is profitable at the end of the session.
8. Trade this approach in active markets only.

Here (Figures 8.5–8.6) are some illustrations of this method using several active stocks and futures:

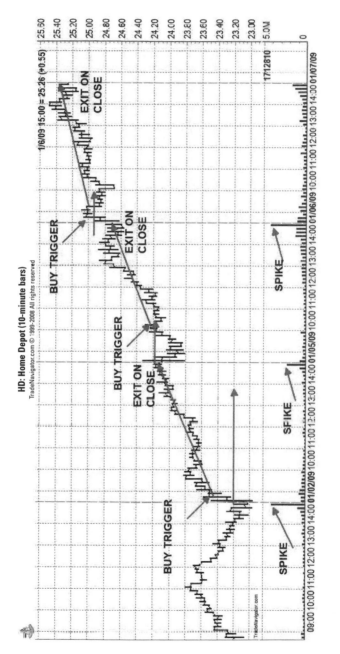

Figure 8.5. Volume spikes and buy triggers, Home Depot stock, ten-minute bars.

147

TESTING THE VOLUME SPIKE SCENARIO

Not all markets show volume spike patterns consistently. I suggest you search through a number of candidates until you find those that exhibit the spike pattern consistently and then do some back testing. Also, remember that not all triggers are buy triggers. Figure 8.7 shows a sell trigger.

Like all other trading techniques, the volume spike method works better in some markets than others, and will require some testing and fine-tuning to get the best results. It is a relatively simple trading method. In Chapters 9, 10, and 11, we turn to more complex technical methods: the convergence/divergence indicators and their use in tandem with other indicators.

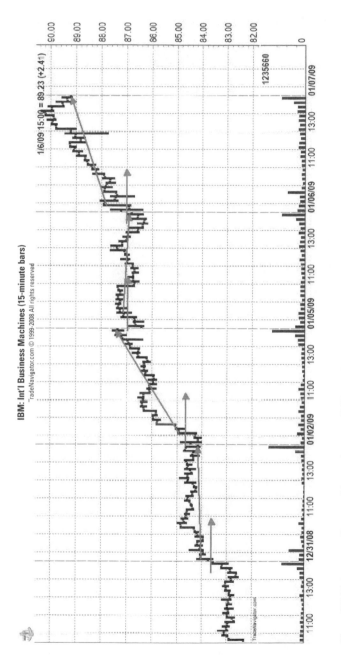

Figure 8.6. Volume spikes and buy triggers, IBM stock, fifteen-minute bars.

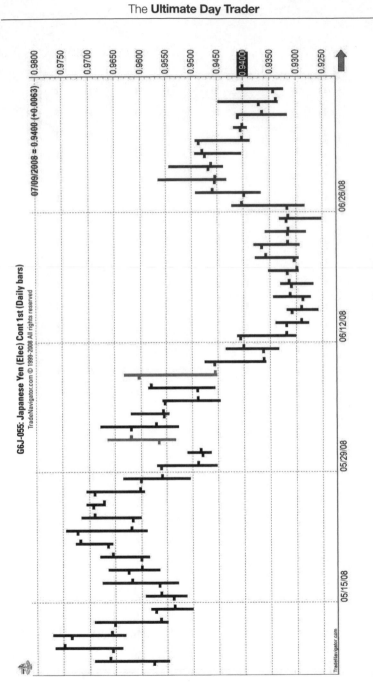

Figure 8.7. Volume spike and sell trigger, ten-year T-note futures, sixty-minute bars.

Chapter **9**

Day Trading with Divergences: Set-Up

Divergence is a popular term among traders. Simply
stated, it refers to a Set-Up method that identifies
potential trading opportunities. It does so by selecting
markets that show an anomalous relationship between
price and a technical indicator. For our purposes
we will use two indicators in order to find and trade
based on divergence. The two indicators are 28-period
Momentum and the moving average convergence
divergence, or MACD, indicator, with a 9 and 18
setting. Here is a brief explanation of each indicator.

THE MOMENTUM INDICATOR

Momentum is a very simple and easily calculated technical tool. Note here that *momentum* (MOM) and the often-used term *rate of change* (ROC) are really both the same indicator, although they are derived using different mathematical operations. In order to calculate the ten-day Momentum of a stock, simply subtract today's price from the price ten days ago. The result is the ten-day MOM. If today's price is $77 and the price ten days ago was $78, then the ten-day Momentum is −1. If today's price is $77 and the price ten days ago was $75, then today's ten-day Momentum is +2.

Momentum is a rate change indicator. It provides us with an idea of trend strength. When Momentum is moving down very quickly, it is an indication that prices are changing rapidly on the down side with large price movements. When Momentum is rising rapidly, it is an indication that the market is trending strongly higher.

Momentum can be used as a trading indicator by applying some simple rules. The first of these is:

1. **Momentum and price tend to move together.** In other words, the **normal** relationship between price and Momentum is for them to exhibit parallel trends, essentially similar times for highs and similar times for lows. They are in synch most of the time; at least they **should be** in synch. Figure 9.1 shows a "normal" relationship between MOM and price.

The other part of the Momentum method, the MACD (Moving Average Convergence Divergence), consists of two

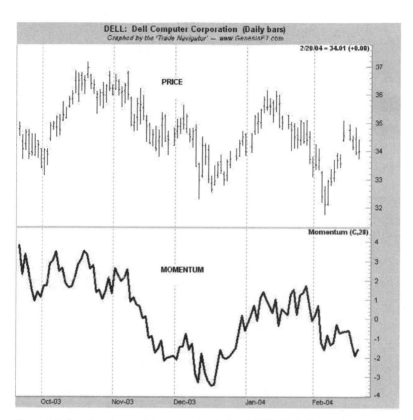

Figure 9.1. Stock price and twenty-eight-day MOM, Dell Computer.

exponential moving averages, which are subtracted from each other. We then compute an exponential moving average of this difference. Typical use of the MACD method triggers buy and sell signals when the MAs cross. For our work we will only use the one line MACD (i.e., the difference between two exponential moving averages). I'll discuss the MACD in much greater detail below.

As you can see from Figure 9.1, Momentum and price tend to move together. However, looking at the end of the chart, you can also see that this is not always the case.

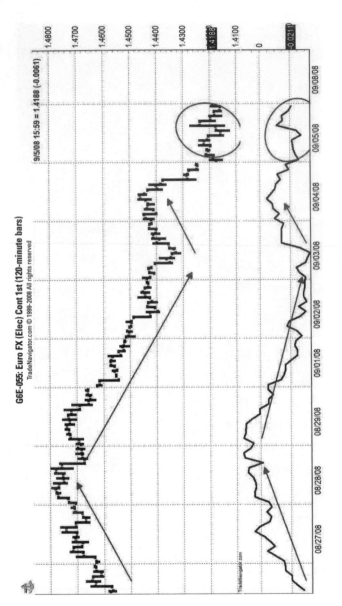

Figure 9.2. Bullish divergence, MOM twenty-eight-day, chart Euro FX, 120-minute bars. Note that the price versus Momentum relationships are all normal until the end of the chart (circled areas at far right). In this case we have *bullish* divergence since price made a new low and Momentum did not.

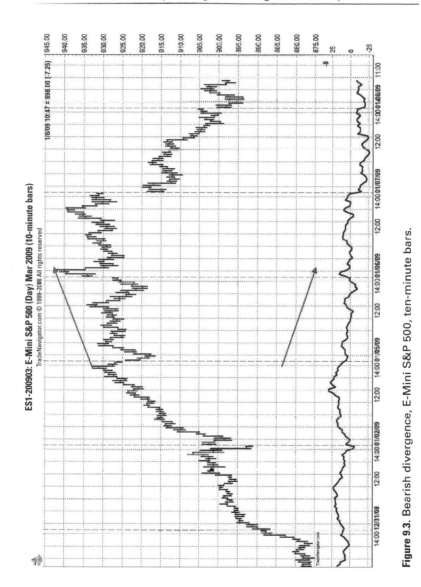

Figure 9.3. Bearish divergence, E-Mini S&P 500, ten-minute bars.

The relationship between price and Momentum is valid in all time frames. The analysis of MOM as an indicator looks for situations where the actual price and the MOM indicator diverge; that is, where the price goes one way and the indicator goes the other. For instance, a *bullish divergence* occurs when the price hits a new low but the Momentum indicator does not, suggesting that the price is temporarily lower than the Momentum suggests it should be. Figure 9.2, for example shows the twenty-eight day period Momentum on an intra-day chart.

A *bearish divergence* occurs when the price is increasing but the MOM indicator shows a decline. This is shown in Figure 9.3

MOMENTUM AS A TRADING METHOD

My many years of trading have led me to the development of what I call the *momentum divergence timing method.* This method can also be used with MACD (to be illustrated later). I believe that Momentum is an excellent indicator that can prove very valuable either as an adjunct to a multi-indicator for your trading system or as part of its own trading system. However, as a timing method on its own it has considerable value.

What follows in this chapter is a discussion of a particular methodology that employs Momentum as its basic timing indicator and combined with specific risk management principles in order to help you develop a total trading approach. I believe that if you use Momentum in a thorough and comprehensive fashion, which includes a disciplined application of the rules and principles to be discussed shortly, it can become your best overall indicator for profits in the stock and commodity markets.

Lest you think that I am proposing Momentum as the "Holy Grail" of stock and commodity trading, rest assured that I am not so naive to believe such a "perfect" approach exists. The methodology that will be taught in this manual is powerful but it is nevertheless still subject to the same limitations as all trading systems and methods.

REMINDER: THE TRADER IS THE WEAKEST LINK

Before explaining the use of divergence as a reminder I want to reiterate my stance on trader psychology and discipline. Here is our second rule:

2. **No matter how profitable the various applications of Momentum and MACD may be, the weakest link in the chain will always be the trader.** It is the trader who will make mistakes. It is the trader who will lose his or her discipline. It is the trader who will find ways to "make" his or her trading system not work.

Finally, it is the trader who will apply the rules presented herein in an inconsistent manner, which will ultimately prove to be the undoing of this or any other method. Ultimately the success or failure of any trading methodology including the one in this manual will be a function of the weakest link in the chain.

We know from a long and expensive experience that systems can be either successful or unsuccessful as a function of the individual who is applying that system. We know that the best system in the hands of an undisciplined trader is a losing system. We also know that a mediocre system used by a disciplined and professional trader can become a winning system.

In order for Momentum or any other method to work, you will first need to understand it, second to apply it, and third to manage the risk effectively.

We will start with a further discussion of the MACD.

MACD

One of the most important tools in the day trader's toolbox, the MACD, or Moving Average Convergence Divergence, consists of two exponential moving averages, which are subtracted from each other. An exponential moving average of this difference is then computed. Typically, the MACD is used to trigger buy and sell signals. This happens when these two exponential moving averages cross. For our work we will use the single-line MACD, which represents the difference between the two exponential moving averages.

There are several "normal" and several "divergent" relationships between Momentum and MACD and price, each of which are important to understand.

PRICE AND MOMENTUM DECLINING TOGETHER (NORMAL)

The typical and normal relationship between Momentum, MACD, and price in a bear market occurs when they are all declining together. As a market moves lower it must have a constant supply of selling pressure. Selling pressure expresses itself as Momentum growing more negative.

Note that when Momentum for a stock declines it does *not* mean that there is less Momentum overall, it means rather that Momentum in the downward direction is *increasing*. If you think of Momentum as energy, then imagine the following: you can drive a car forward or you can drive a car backward. No matter which direction you take you have expended energy to make the car move; Momentum indicates the amount of energy, not the direction. Markets, in my estimation, behave in a similar fashion.

Forget those complicated concepts you've heard about. Concepts like "chaos theory," "regression analysis" and "wave forms." They may be right but they're not the simplest answer to the question of "where are prices going?"

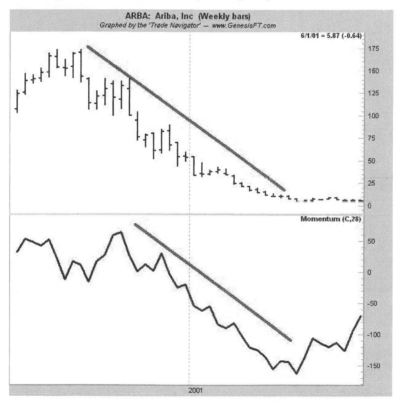

Figure 9.4. Price and Momentum declining in unison, Ariba Inc. stock, weekly bars. This is a normal pattern.

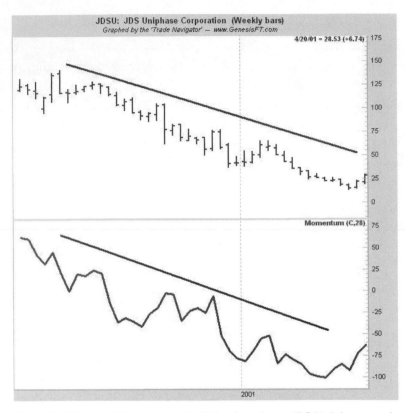

Figure 9.5. Price and Momentum declining in unison, JDS Uniphase stock, weekly bars. This is a normal pattern.

Figures 9.4 and 9.5 show the ideal relationship between declining prices and Momentum becoming more negative. Remember that Momentum can fall below zero. Zero is *not* a stopping point for Momentum. The lower Momentum goes the lower price goes.

Furthermore, as Momentum becomes more negative, prices are likely to continue lower. Declining Momentum with price moving sideways or higher is a bearish indication since

Momentum tends to lead price down as well as up (see the previous section).

It should be noted at this point that there *is* a logical stopping point for declining Momentum. Prices have a downside limit. The lowest price that a market can go to is zero. Naturally Momentum will eventually stop declining when the market price goes to zero. Unless a company is going bankrupt and is being de-listed from trading, there is a good possibility that as the price of a stock approaches zero (or as a commodity price gets very low) Momentum will begin to level off and turn higher. Many excellent buying opportunities in stocks and commodities develop when this occurs—more about this situation in a later chapter.

NORMAL PATTERNS: MOMENTUM AND MACD

Normal patterns are further demonstrated by looking at both the Momentum and MACD indicators in tandem. The next two charts (figures 9.6 and 9.7) show normal patterns exhibited with both Momentum and MACD.

Both of these charts show normal price and indicator patterns. They can be traded based on the idea that a move in a particular direction may be strengthening or weakening. But when price and one or both indicators *diverge*, that condition can signal even greater trading opportunities.

BULLISH DIVERGENCE: PRICES MOVE LOWER AS MOMENTUM MOVES HIGHER

When price and Momentum diverge from one another, or go in opposite directions, it represents a very important trading

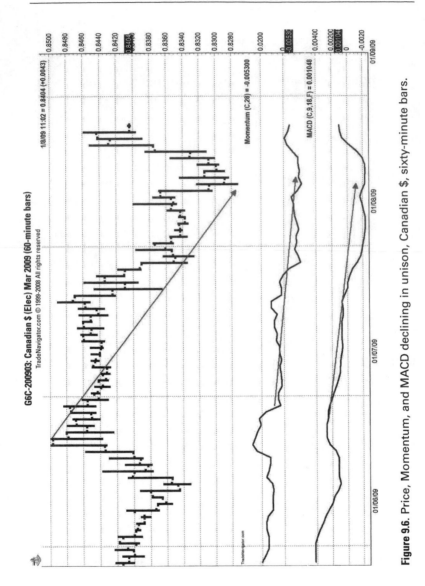

Figure 9.6. Price, Momentum, and MACD declining in unison, Canadian $, sixty-minute bars.

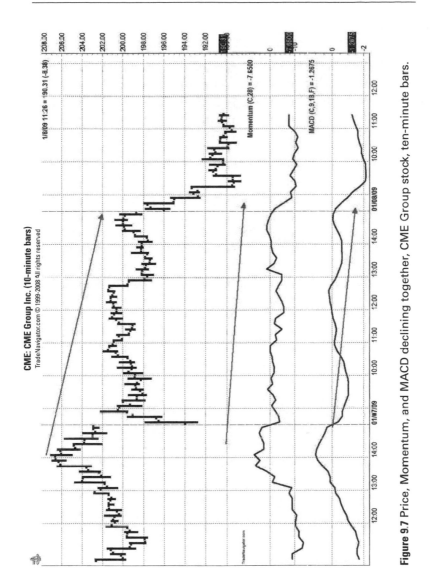

Figure 9.7 Price, Momentum, and MACD declining together, CME Group stock, ten-minute bars.

condition. If Momentum leads price and if Momentum begins to rise while price is moving down then it's a reasonable assumption that at some point in the future the price will move up.

Unless Momentum takes a new tack down, prices will eventually move in the direction of Momentum. When the prices and Momentum begin to move in opposite directions, the market is telling us something important about its intended direction. And we had better listen carefully.

Figures 9.8 and 9.9 illustrate this bullish divergence condition in stocks and futures.

Just as the decline in price accompanied by strengthening Momentum and MACD indicators denotes a bullish divergence and thus a reversal of prices to the upside, the reverse, weakening indicators with a strengthening price is a bearish divergence and foretells a fall in price. This pattern is often seen prior to market tops.

Figures 9.10–9.11 show the bearish divergence in advance of a market top. Please take a few minutes to examine my notes.

The same pattern can be discerned with or without the MACD indicator, as indicated by Figure 9.12.

Figure 9.13 shows a variation on the theme. A new price high, or top, was not confirmed by a Momentum top—another bearish divergence and sell signal.

In figure 9.14 this is a clear standard and clear-cut bearish divergence prior to a top based on Momentum alone.

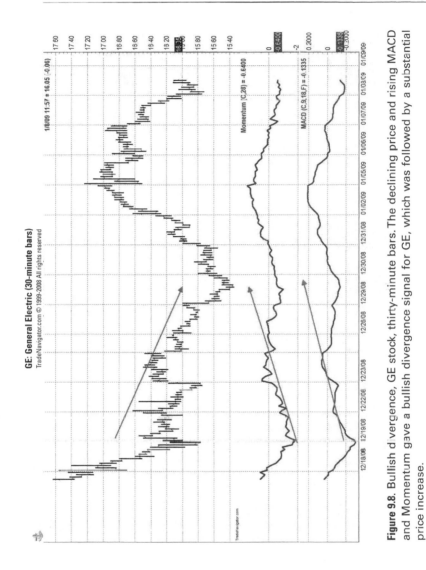

GE: General Electric (30-minute bars)

Figure 9.8. Bullish divergence, GE stock, thirty-minute bars. The declining price and rising MACD and Momentum gave a bullish divergence signal for GE, which was followed by a substantial price increase.

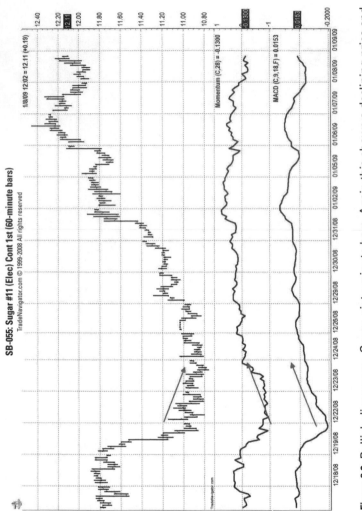

Figure 9.9. Bullish divergence, Sugar, sixty-minute bars. Again this shows a declining price and rising MACD and Momentum. The bullish divergence in sugar futures was followed by a price increase.

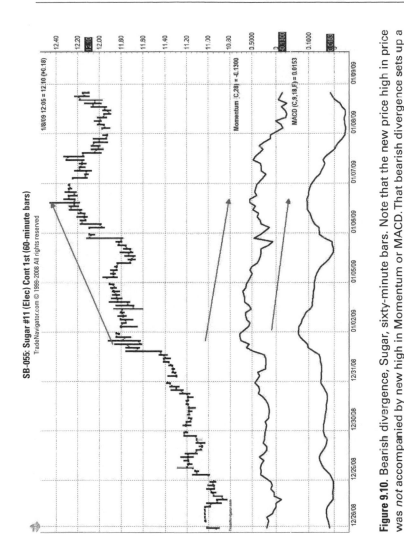

SB-055: Sugar #11 (Elec) Cont 1st (60-minute bars)

Figure 9.10. Bearish divergence, Sugar, sixty-minute bars. Note that the new price high in price was *not* accompanied by new high in Momentum or MACD. That bearish divergence sets up a sell pattern in the form of bearish divergence.

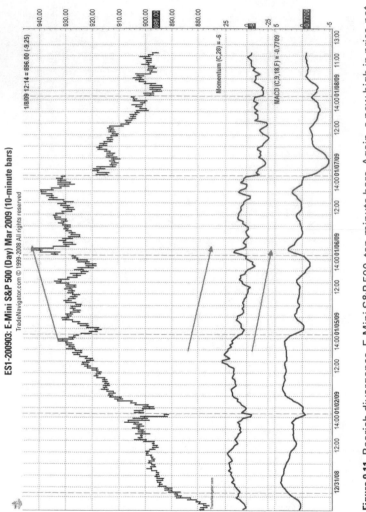

Figure 9.11. Bearish divergence, E-Mini S&P 500, ten-minute bars. Again, a new high in price *not* accompanied by a new high in Momentum or MACD sets up a sell pattern in the form of bearish divergence. Note the large decline that followed the illustrated divergence period.

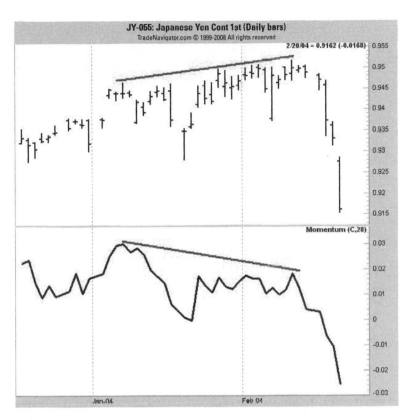

Figure 9.12. Bearish divergence, Japanese Yen futures, daily bars. This figure shows another bearish divergence and sell pattern, based on the Momentum indicator alone. New high in price *not* accompanied by new high in Momentum sets up a sell pattern in the form of bearish divergence.

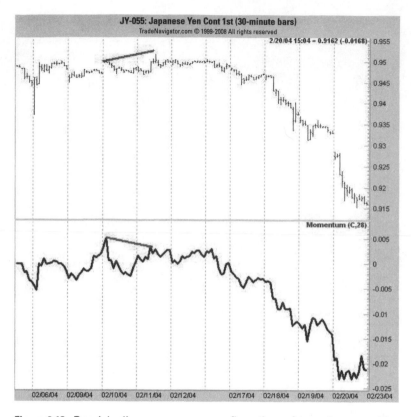

Figure 9.13. Bearish divergence, non-confirmation of top, Japanese Yen futures, thirty-minute bars. Large price decline on intra-day chart following new high in price not accompanied by new high in Momentum.

APPLYING MOMENTUM DIVERGENCE: MY THEORY

There are three essential ingredients to the application of Momentum as part of the methodology that you will learn in this book.

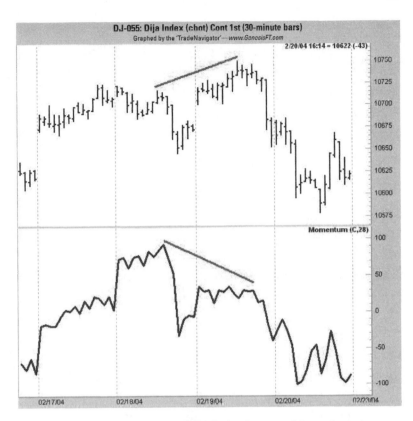

Figure 9.14. Bearish divergence, DJIA Index futures, thirty minute bars.

1. Recognize the existence of bullish and/or bearish divergence.
2. Determine the presence or absence of a buy or sell signal.
3. Effectively manage risk and profit once a trade has been initiated based on a momentum divergence buy or sell signal.

I will spend a little time discussing my understanding of what momentum tells us about a market at any given point in time. Inasmuch as Momentum is a measure of the internal strength or weakness of a market, we can use it to determine very easily at any point how weak or strong a market is. Moreover, we can frequently tell when a market is about to turn higher or lower, based on the behavior of its Momentum indicator.

In order to truly understand where a market is going, it is imperative to understand who is in "control" of that market. When I use the term "control" I am not referring to a group of individuals who are conspiring or plotting to manipulate or "corner" a given market. Rather I mean control in the sense of traders having an impact on a market.

As an example, consider the following situation. There are 1,000 traders actively involved in a feeder cattle market. Seven hundred of the actively involved traders are buyers who believe that prices are going to go higher. If they act upon their expectations, and they have a sufficient amount of money behind them, they can readily overcome all of the selling pressure that is being applied by the other 300 traders, who may be bearish on the market. In this case the bulls are in control of the market.

The degree of control in a market depends not only on the size of the bull and bear groups of traders, but also upon the strength of the bullish or bearish sentiment by the various groups of traders. Assume that a particular market or stock has been moving lower for many weeks. As long as the fundamental conditions underlying the supply and demand factors for that market remain negative, that market will continue to move lower.

Although the price of that market may continue to go down as traders sell the market based on yesterday's news, knowledgeable traders (or if you prefer "insiders") will begin to buy that market or stock, strongly convinced of an eventual change of trend. Although the price of the market may still be going down, Momentum will begin to move in a different direction, and the end result will be bullish divergence. In other words *price continues to move lower while Momentum moves higher.* Eventually a tipping point will occur in which the bulls gain control over the bears and prices begin to move higher.

Conversely, a very typical situation in terms of market tops occurs while prices are still moving higher based upon public interpretations of supposedly bullish fundamentals. While the public is still buying and prices are moving higher, professional traders are liquidating long positions and selling short. In such situations, prices often continue to move higher while Momentum moves lower.

This condition can only continue for a certain amount of time before a significant trend change develops and prices go down, either due to a lack of buying and or to a significant amount of selling. This condition is reflected by bearish divergence between price and Momentum. What you will see in this case is prices continuing to move higher as Momentum continues to move lower. When the balance of power shifts and the sellers outnumber the buyers, the market will change direction. Divergences setup by Momentum, and MACD indicators, are thus *leading* indicators, which in most cases are effective trade Set-Up and Triggers. You'll find over time that the moves foretold by these indicators can be quite large in either direction.

Note that in the above method, savvy traders are *not* trading the news—as I discuss in a later chapter, such an approach brings numerous perils with it. Rather, traders who focus on Momentum and MACD indicators are taking a quantitative, objective approach to the market. Such a method is far more likely to yield positive results than one based on the random ups and downs of the news cycle.

Once you learn to recognize the buy and sell signals you'll find it relatively easy to spot moves within various time frames that are frequently quite large in either direction.

This is in no way a guarantee, however, that by simply being able to spot these moves you will be successful in trading the stock or commodity markets. To do that, you must combine an understanding of the Momentum and MACD indicators with effective money management.

MOMENTUM IS A LEADING INDICATOR TIMING THE TRADE

As I explained in the previous section, leading indicators tend to be more effective than lagging indicators inasmuch as they are frequently not as vulnerable to market whipsaws as are trend-following systems. In examining the charts contained in this chapter as well as the charts that you study on your own, you'll find that Momentum tends to lead price most of the time. Frequently you'll find that if a market is declining while Momentum is rising, shortly thereafter prices will begin to rise.

Conversely you'll find that if prices are rising while Momentum is falling, prices will eventually turn lower. The important factor in using any leading indicator is that it must not get you into the market too early, for you may have to sit through some significant movements against you before your trade becomes profitable. In some ways this is or can be just as bad as getting into a trade too late. It is therefore important for Momentum to validate its divergence signals by the use of a specific timing indicator, which will theoretically factor out incorrect trades.

Momentum divergence is the key to the divergence method. If you understand how to spot Momentum divergence you will be two-thirds of the way there. The other part of the story is timing. Chapter 10 will discuss specific timing triggers for Momentum and MACD divergence.

Chapter **10**

Day Trading with Divergence: Momentum Timing Triggers

This chapter is designed to familiarize you with the *divergence timing method.* As you know from what was discussed in previous chapters, Momentum divergence can be either bullish or bearish. Bullish Momentum divergence often develops prior to a pricc low, while bearish Momentum divergence often develops prior to a price high. Importantly, however, you must also remember that not all highs and lows are preceded by bullish or bearish divergence signals. And not all turns in market trends are preceded by bullish or bearish divergence signals.

177

In a later chapter we will see how you can spot turns in market trends that are not preceded by bullish or bearish divergence and which do not give divergence buy or sell signals. But they are *not* part of the divergence method.

Before we consider these turns, however, let's examine specific divergence buy signals and how to determine them. After that, we will discuss several exit strategies. In order for you to understand the basic divergence timing method, it will be necessary for you to follow me through a few simple steps. Do not get frustrated. Perseverance will pay off!

Learning any new trading system or method is like learning a new language. In developing skills with Momentum and MACD-based trading, you'll need to forget many of the things you have learned about timing.

Practice is very important in this or any other method. I've provided you with many practice charts and numerous examples. Use them. Once you have learned the divergence method you will have learned a new language that I believe will serve you well both in the short run and in the long run. I can't stress enough that in order to succeed with divergence, you need to practice, practice, and practice. The more charts you study, the more you will understand what's involved. You will be able to spot divergence signals within seconds of examining the charts.

IDENTIFYING DIVERGENCE BUY SIGNALS

In order for you to spot divergence buy signals you must remember the bullish Momentum concept. Remember that the mere presence of bullish Momentum divergence does not immediately trigger a divergence buy signal. In fact—this is important—Momentum divergence can remain in a bullish condition for many weeks or months without a buy signal being triggered.

On occasion the bullish Momentum divergence will not only fail to develop into a buy signal but may, in fact, turn into a bearish pattern without a buy signal having been triggered. In some cases Momentum divergence can continue bullish for an extended period of time without a buy signal developing while prices continue lower. This is an essential fact about divergence. Remember: *The presence of bullish Momentum divergence does not necessarily mean that there will be a buy signal.*

Conversely the presence of bearish Momentum divergence does not automatically trigger a sell signal. In every case the most important thing for you to remember is that timing is of the essence. Timing must confirm all bullish Momentum divergence and all bearish Momentum in divergence in order for them to develop into trading signals.

Thus, it goes almost without saying that to act prematurely by buying on bullish Momentum divergence without divergence buy signals is contrary to the rules. Likewise to act prematurely and sell on bearish Momentum divergence without divergence sell signals is a mistake. To do so will likely get you into trouble. I have provided numerous chart examples illustrating bullish divergence (and bearish divergence) patterns in the previous chapter. Please study them carefully.

It is impossible for me to stress too strongly the point I have made in the last several paragraphs. Write above your computer the following rule:

Bullish Momentum divergence in itself is not a buy signal!

If bullish Momentum divergence isn't in itself a buy signal, then what is? I will first explain the divergence buy signal, then show you a number of illustrations as well as offer a step-by-step procedure to guide you through this complex territory.

CHOOSING THE BUY POINT AFTER BULLISH MOMENTUM DIVERGENCE

First, you must identify a period of bullish Momentum divergence. That is, you must find a period of time during which prices move lower and create new lows. If, at the same time Momentum is moving higher and shows higher lows, that generates a buy signal. To repeat: *A buy signal is generated when, in any given time frame, a new closing Momentum high is created that is higher than the highest Momentum during the period of bullish convergence.*

I'm sure that you followed that perfectly! Oh . . . you didn't?

I can make it much simpler for you if you take a look at Figure 10.1. This shows the following pattern: A new low in price was made at point A, possibly a market bottom. At approximately the same time, at point B, Momentum was not making a new low. Look to the left of point B. You can see that there was a lower Momentum point. This is the classic bullish divergence pattern.

Although price made a new low for the move, Momentum did not. On my chart I have marked the new price low within the corresponding Momentum to that price low with B. I have also marked the previous Momentum low with a C and the corresponding price with a D. *Point E is our buy point.*

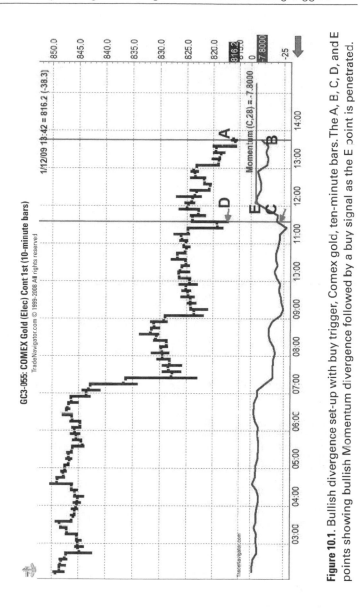

GC3-D55: COMEX Gold (Elec) Cont 1st (10-minute bars)
TradeNavigator.com © 1999-2008 All rights reserved

1/12/09 13:42 = 816.2 (-38.3)

Momentum (C,28) = -7.8000

Figure 10.1. Bullish divergence set-up with buy trigger, Comex gold, ten-minute bars. The A, B, C, D, and E points showing bullish Momentum divergence followed by a buy signal as the E point is penetrated.

Although price made a new low for the move, Momentum did not. So at that point in time, the buy isn't triggered. On my chart I have marked the new price low within the corresponding Momentum to that price low with B. I have also marked the previous Momentum low with a C and the corresponding price with a D. These four points mark the bullish divergence.

Then, the price level represented by Point E would be the *buy* trigger, or buy point—when the Momentum indicator rises to this level once again the buy is triggered. Note that the trigger is tripped at the end of the price bar, or time frame—firing the trade before the end can be premature, especially when long time periods are in use.

This example illustrates the concept that I presented with regard to the selection of bullish divergence. Bullish divergence can be easily spotted once you have sufficient experience in doing so. Just remember that there are a number of rules that you must follow if you are going to be successful in finding periods of bullish divergence. Here is a synopsis:

1. For spotting bullish divergence on daily charts, use a three-month timing window. The three-month window will give the best indications of what is and what isn't a bullish divergence pattern for that market, during which you will spot or attempt to spot the bullish divergence. You may use up to five or six months once you become experienced with the technique. However, the sixty-price bar window is sufficient for you to find valid signals. Do not use periods of time that are shorter than three months in order for you to develop a bullish divergence time frame. This does not mean that the bullish (or bearish) divergence doesn't occur over the entire three-month time frame; rather, it

typically sets up several times during the period that the bullish divergence must occur. You are simply using the three-month period as your frame of reference.

2. In order for a valid bullish divergence signal to occur, the period of bullish divergence must have been at least six calendar days or, in other words, six trading days (or six price bars on charts that are less than or more than daily). This holds true if you are using intra-day charts as well. If for example you are using an intra-day time frame of sixty-minute charts, you will still require at least six of those hourly bars in order to develop a period of bullish divergence. You will find this more clearly shown in the illustrations that follow.

Now here's the step-by-step method I promised you earlier for finding the buy trigger. You can practice this extensively on charts until you get the hang of it.

1. Find the lowest price low on the chart. Once this price low, the potential bottom, has been found, mark it with the letter "A."

2. Now move to the Momentum indicator and mark the current Momentum indicator position accordingly with the letter "B."

3. From this point, move to the previous Momentum low and mark it "C."

4. Move to the price that corresponds to C and mark it with a D. You should now have a configuration looking like Figure 10.1.

5. Look for a buy signal, or "E" point. Once you have selected your points A, B, C and D, you are ready to draw your

penetration point, which will yield the buy signal. This is the E, buy, point.

CHOOSING THE BUY POINT

The buy point on Momentum is always the highest point between the two Momentum points that you chose when you evaluated the bullish divergence situation. On your charts, use E to mark this point. I will also call it the Momentum Breakout Point (MBP).

CHOOSING THE SELL POINT AFTER BEARISH MOMENTUM DIVERGENCE

The Momentum divergence sell point is analogous to a buy point, but of course, everything is occurring in the opposite direction. First, the Momentum divergence shows an increasing price but a decreasing Momentum indicator. Then, draw in the points and lines again, as A, B, C, D and E as above, the "E" being the *low* Momentum point between the two charted Momentum points C and B inclusive. When the Momentum indicator penetrates that level again, it is a sell trigger, or sell signal.

Figure 10.2 shows how this pattern develops. As you can see, the procedure is simple, mechanical in nature, and totally objective.

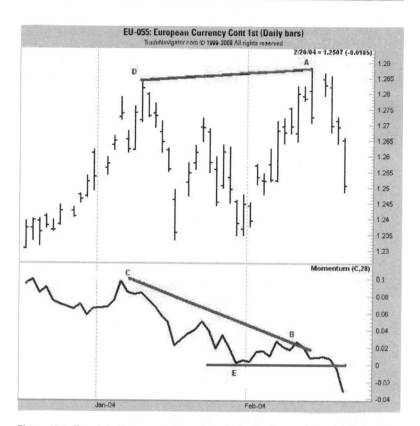

Figure 10.2. Bearish divergence set-up with sell trigger, Euro futures, daily bars. The chart shows an ideal bearish divergence A, B, C, D, E Momentum pattern. The "A" is the market top; the sell is triggered when the Momentum line penetrates the level defined by point E.

REVIEWING DIVERGENCE

Not surprisingly, there are a lot of important things to remember about the divergence method. The following are worth noting:

- **Not all divergences occur at tops or bottoms, and not all tops or bottoms show divergence.** Many major tops and bottoms in all time frames develop as divergence patterns; however, note that *not* all tops and bottoms are accompanied by divergence. I would estimate that about 60 percent to 70 percent of meaningful tops and bottoms develop with divergence patterns.
- **Follow your charts consistently**. The key to using the divergence method is to consistently follow your charts and indicators. Some charting software packages can be programmed to identify divergence patterns as they develop. These can be a great help when you attempt to find important divergence patterns as they develop.
- **Lock in profits with trailing stops**. Another vital aspect of success with the divergence approach is to use the trailing stop procedure to lock in profits.
- **Remember that divergence is not a trading system**. It is, rather, a trading methodology incorporating some subjectivity; it does require some degree of judgment, but that does not negate its ability and power.
- **Like other methods, divergence requires discipline**. As in the case of all trading methods, your success will be a function of your discipline and attention as a trader. If you allow yourself to fall behind in your studies and analyses or if you lose your discipline when it comes

time to place trades, then divergence will not work for you. Nor, for that matter, will any other system or method.

The weakest link in the chain is the trader. This has always been the case and will probably always be the case.

LEARNING BY EXAMPLE

I'll close this chapter with five more fairly clear-cut examples of divergence showing bottoms and tops (figures 10.3–10.7). The A, B, C, D charting method works for all; the "E" penetrating line is also shown.

Now that we have examined the three-step process in establishing Set-Ups and Triggers, we will look at Follow-Through. The next chapter will discuss several Follow-Through methods.

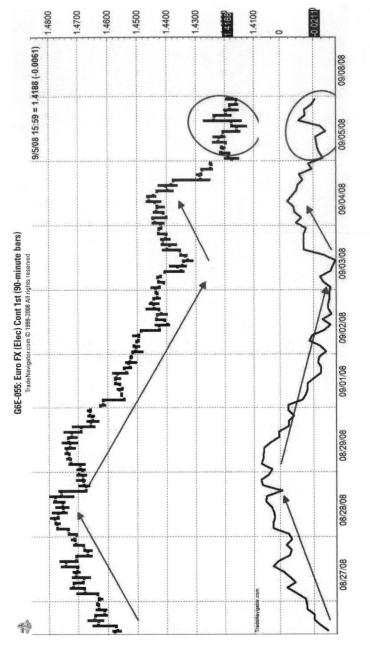

G6E-055: Euro FX (Elec) Cont 1st (90-minute bars)

9/5/08 15:59 = 1.4188 (-0.0061)

Figure 10.3. Bullish divergence, set-up with buy trigger, E-Mini S&P 500, ninety-minute bars.

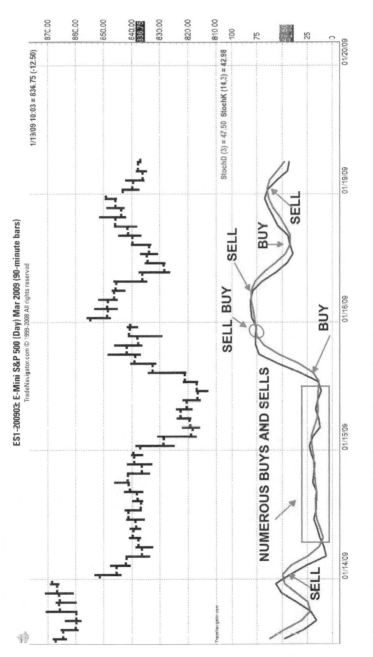

ES1-200903 E-Mini S&P 500 (Day) Mar 2009 (90-minute bars)

1/13/09 10:03 = 836.75 (-12.50)

StochD (3) = 47.50 StochK (14,3) = 42.98

Figure 10.4. Set-up and Trigger E-Mini (Day), ninety-minute bars.

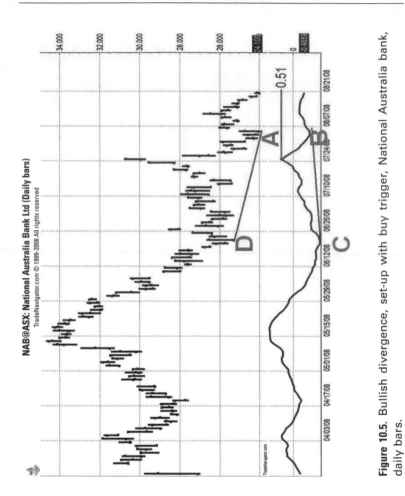

NAB@ASX: National Australia Bank Ltd (Daily bars)

Figure 10.5. Bullish divergence, set-up with buy trigger, National Australia bank, daily bars.

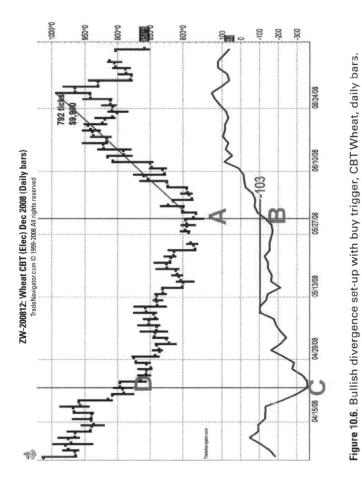

Figure 10.6. Bullish divergence set-up with buy trigger, CBT Wheat, daily bars.

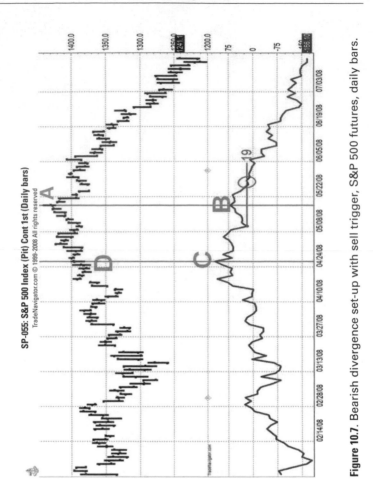

SP-055: S&P 500 Index (Pit) Cont 1st (Daily bars)

Figure 10.7. Bearish divergence set-up with sell trigger, S&P 500 futures, daily bars.

Chapter **11**

Day Trading With Divergence: Follow-Through

Once you are able to find divergence set-ups

and triggers using either the MACD and/or the

momentum divergence methods as described in

the preceding two chapters, it's time to put your

knowledge into practice. As a day trader your decisions

must be fast, implemented quickly, and you must exit

trades before the end of the trading day. Here we

finish the process by examining the follow-through on

divergence trades.

I have previously emphasized the fact that market entry for day trading should be 100 percent objective. Market entry must be specific, and we must follow the operational procedures. On the other hand, market exit cannot and should not be 100 percent mechanical due to the fact that exits must be completed by the end of the trading day. I have been in the trading business long enough to know that many traders will disagree with me. They will claim that exits as well as entries must be totally mechanical. I do not believe that the accuracy of trading systems and methods allows for a totally objective exit strategy without limiting profits. Hence, I have developed a hybrid methodology that consists of the following general procedures:

- Establish and implement purely objective entry rules.
- Establish and implement purely objective exit rules as a first profit target.
- Establish and implement purely objective risk and or stop loss procedures.
- Implement a "danger zone" strategy. This strategy exits a position at a first profit target and then removes most of the dollar risk by following up with stop losses at break even.
- If not stopped out, implement a number of possible alternative exit strategies as well as the possibility of holding a part of your position beyond the end of the day.

Following this method, one of the following three scenarios will occur:

1. You will have a profit target that allows you to "take some money off the table," which thereby mitigates your potential loss.
2. You will be able to reduce risk effectively to zero once the first target has been hit, which will allow you to ride a "free trade."
3. You will have the flexibility to exit part of your position in any of several different ways.

DON'T FORGET THE "DANGER ZONE" CONCEPT

If you recall from what I have presented earlier in this book, the danger zone is simply my way of saying that until you have reached a first profit target on a day trade (or for that matter a trade of any time length) you are in danger of taking a loss based on your initial stop loss or risk. I am a firm believer in the "free trade" concept. Simply stated, the sooner we make a trade—or any portion thereof—"free" the better.

A free trade is a trade that is essentially without risk. It is a trade that we can hold for a profit without the fear of having it turn into a loss (unless there is an unexpected gap or bad price execution). The good news is that by riding the free trade we have exposure to large profits. The bad news is that we may be stopped out many times at the break-even stop and thereby give up some of the potential profit on our last position. I strongly suggest that the more often you can get into the free trade zone the more likely you are to capture the large profits on the last position.

It's like football, where a defensive foul happens when the ball is snapped; the play is free unless it's blown dead. The sooner we can get out of the danger zone, the sooner we are able to take some profit, but, more importantly, the sooner we can enjoy the benefits of riding a free trade.

With all of the above in mind, let's take a look at a few trades that put the divergence Set-Up, Trigger, and Follow-Through into practice. After all, theory and the written word are essentially useless to traders unless the methods and procedures can be put into action. Here are some specific examples that illustrate the day trade procedures for MACD and Momentum divergence.

It takes only one of the two, Momentum or MACD, to trigger a trade. We watch both, and whichever method triggers first is the one we use for our trade entry and exit strategy.

Here is a list of abbreviations used on the charts that follow:

- B = divergence buy trigger
- S = divergence sell trigger
- A, B, C, D = divergence setup points
- E = divergence trigger point
- P1 = first profit target
- P2 = full profit target
- X = end of day exit
- TSX = trailing stop exit

GETTING STARTED—TIME FRAMES AND TRADE SIZE

First, you must determine the time frame in which you want to day trade:

- For futures such as S&P, I recommend no less than the five-minute time frame using the day session data.
- For currency futures and/or FOREX, use two-hour or even four-hour charts to overcome the narrow bar tendency during off-peak hours.
- For other futures markets and for stocks, use either the five-minute, ten-minute, or thirty-minute charts for the day session only, depending on trading volume and/or price range.
- If you day trade lower priced active stocks, then you will need to compensate for commission costs and lower profit potential by using larger positions.

From here, let's jump right into some examples.

TRADING WITH DIVERGENCE

The following three scenarios illustrate "real world" trading—or non-trading if the conditions don't support it—with divergence.

Figure 11.1 shows a three-hour Euro currency futures with MACD and Momentum. There is a setup but no trigger. A trigger will occur if and when the "E" point on either of the two indicators has been penetrated, but that doesn't happen within the time frame of this chart.

Important: Please note that a trigger can only occur at the *end* of a price bar. During the course of a price bar the trigger point may be penetrated frequently. It is only at the end of the price bar that a trigger is valid. Please don't "jump the gun" by

197

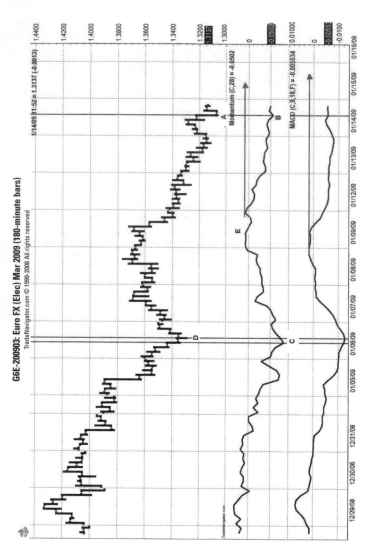

Figure 11.1. Set-up, no trigger, Euro, 180-minute bars.

executing a trade before the end of the bar since this would be a clear violation of the rules that I have developed and presented to you in this book.

Some traders regularly break the rules and this proves to be their undoing. At the risk of repeating myself, *breaking the rules will teach you "bad behaviors" that will eventually (more likely sooner rather than later) lead to confusion.* Confusion will lead to inconsistency. Inconsistency will lead to lack of discipline. Lack of discipline will lead to losses. Enough said.

Now let's move on to a complete set of signals and a complete trade.

Figure 11.2 is a five-minute day session Treasury Bond chart showing divergence sell signal and exits. The setup occurred at points A, B, C, and D. The trigger point F was penetrated one price bar after the high of the move. A short position would have been taken at the signal. The first target, P1, was one half the range of the highest price high and lowest price low during the time frame from A to D inclusive. After P1 was hit, partial profits would have been taken, with additional profits taken at and when P2 was hit; these are subjective decisions.

After P2 was hit, a trailing stop procedure would have been implemented. Exit would be at the end of the day (point X). The trade could have been held until the next opening and exited at that time using the first profitable opening (FPO) strategy. Alternatively the trade could be held with a trailing stop procedure. The trade would have been stopped out when the market rallied.

Figure 11.3 shows multiple setups and triggers. This is a five-minute chart of Google showing a completed trade as well as two additional set-ups and triggers, all in the same day. It is not unusual to see several signals within the course of a day using

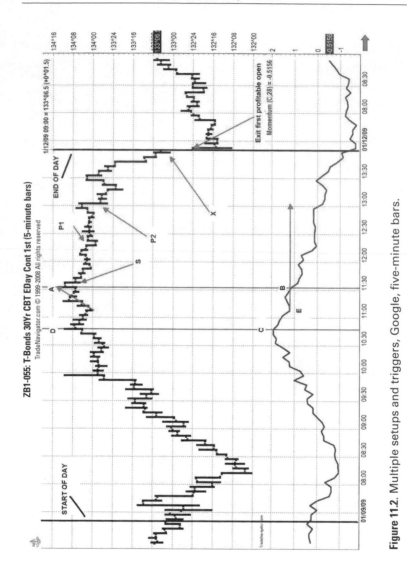

Figure 11.2. Multiple setups and triggers, Google, five-minute bars.

the five-minute chart on higher-priced stocks. In this case, there were two more divergence set-up and trigger signals on MACD, both profitable by the end of the day.

ADDITIONAL POINTERS

The charts in this chapter illustrated the Set-Up, Trigger, and Follow-Through method for Momentum and MACD divergence. Note that there are some critical elements to consider before you begin using this method. They are as follows:

Volume is important. The stock, FOREX, or futures markets you select for your day trades must have sufficient trading volume to allow prompt entry and exit at or near the bid or offer price. If you attempt to use "at the market" orders in a thinly traded (i.e., low volume) market, then your price executions will be poor, and you may lose money when you should have made money.

• **Trade active markets only**. Following the last point, it's a good idea to restrict your day trading to active markets only. A good working definition of "active" markets in stocks is at least 5 million shares average daily volume for the last ten trading sessions. In futures, I like to see at least 10,000 contracts average daily volume for the last ten trading sessions. In both cases more is better. Trading volume figures for the FOREX markets are not available, so tread lightly there and monitor price executions closely to see if the pair you are trading is viable.

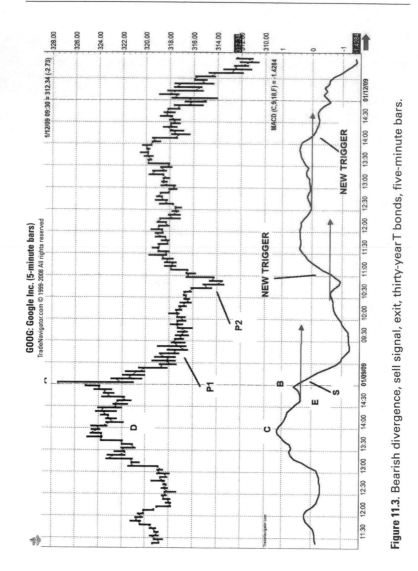

GOOG: Google Inc. (5-minute bars)

Figure 11.3. Bearish divergence, sell signal, exit, thirty-yearT bonds, five-minute bars.

- **Pay attention not just to volume but also to range.** Choose your day trading markets based on daily price range in addition to trading volume. A stock or commodity with a large average daily price range will give you more opportunities for profit. Hence, higher-priced stocks and/or futures markets that have a large tick value will be good candidates for your day trading activities. You can trade lower-priced securities and smaller ranges, but will have to trade larger positions to make it worth while.

Having said this, it should be noted that this is not the only way to go. You can select lower priced stocks and lower tick value commodities. (Tick value is, of course, the monetary value of a one-increment move in the given commodity.) for day trading but you will want to trade larger positions in order to make the game worth while.

Brokerage firms may vary in their policy or policies regarding day trading and margin requirements. While there are clear legal rules, there are also some differences between firms.

You are best off using an electronic order entry format for day trading. This will circumvent the need to deal with an actual broker, which will undoubtedly save you time and money.

- **Be selective and consistent in your day trade choices using the divergence method.** Once you have selected some candidates for day trades using divergence, you will be best off using the same markets rather than jumping from one market to another.

- **Don't trade too many positions**. Do not attempt to trade too many divergence situations at the same time unless you are extremely organized or you have a trading partner. If you try to day trade too many markets at the same time you will miss trades and/or you will make mistakes.
- **Use both indicators**. Remember that we use two indicators for divergence: MACD 9, 18, and Momentum 28. A Set-Up and/or a Trigger on either indicator constitutes a valid entry signal. We do not need both to confirm.

Finally, remember that there is art as well as science to day trading. The way in which you exit profitable trades can make the difference between profits and losses. You must always attempt to maximize profits. I have given you a number of ideas and methods as to how this goal may be achieved.

This chapter concludes our study of divergence-based trading; in the next chapter we move on to another technical indicator of price behavior, the *stochastic indicator*.

Chapter **12**

The Stochastic "POP" Method

A number of years ago my friend, the late George

Lane, popularized what's known as the *stochastic*

indicator. He attracted an ardent group of followers

who soon came to believe that the new trend indicator

was the Holy Grail of stock and commodity trading.

Although there is no denying that George's work was groundbreaking and that the stochastic indicator (SI) was indeed a powerful tool, it has considerable drawbacks. George acknowledged the limitations of his indicator. He was realistic in his assessment of its value. However, that didn't prevent thousands of traders from attempting to implement the SI in ways that he never recommended or developed. This is not an unusual situation in the use of technical market tools.

The stochastic POP is so named because markets have shown a tendency to surge higher or to "pop" higher or to drop sharply or "pop" lower when a given condition of the stochastic indicator develops.

As in the case of many market tools, the SI looks good on a chart. However, it has a tendency to be late in spotting trend changes. Therefore it qualifies as a lagging indicator. Without a doubt the SI is capable of letting traders know approximately when prices are topping or bottoming or when prices are supposedly "overbought" or "oversold." I place quotation marks around these terms because I consider them to be essentially useless if not, in fact, counterproductive. I believe that thinking in terms of overbought or oversold can lead you to costly errors. Reliance on them will lead you to miss potentially winning trades and stay with losing trades for too long. SI can be a powerful tool, but it must be used very selectively.

WHAT IS SI?

Simply stated, SI is a rate of change indicator that is normalized on a percentage scale to provide a reading of 0 to 100. It is a very simple indicator, which does not require a great deal of mathematical expertise. Virtually every contemporary charting and/or technical analysis computer program or website offers SI as one of their indicators. SI consists of two parallel indicators.

1. The main line, or %K line, is sometimes referred to as the "fast" stochastic oscillator. It typically calculates the ratio of two closing price statistics: the difference between the latest closing price and the lowest price in the last N days over the difference between the highest and lowest prices in the last N days. The value of N is typically fourteen days.

2. The signal line, sometimes called the slow stochastic indicator or %D line, is a moving average of the %K line.

Stochastic lines operate on a scale between 0 and 100 and show where a security's price closed relative to its high: If the SI closes a period at its high, it's 100, if at its low, it's 0.

Both K and D lines are plotted in a manner similar to the Momentum or MACD indicators. When they cross a certain threshold or cross over each other, buy and sell signals are generated.

There are numerous variations in how these two readings are calculated. The problem is that the consistency of the SI application is undermined by the fact that there is no standardized formula. The stochastic indicator is a standard part of many day trading software packages now, but it seems as if every software vendor has made a slight variation in the calculation methodology. This, of course, has caused an understandable degree of confusion. The SI reading that you may get from your software program may differ considerably from mine, even though we may both be looking at a 14-period SI.

As you can well imagine, this also creates havoc when one tries to back-test results of the SI.

I mentioned earlier my dislike of the terms "overbought" and "oversold." Before presenting details of my preferred SI method for day trading, let's examine the "overbought"/ "oversold" concept.

THE FALLACY OF "OVERBOUGHT" (OB) AND "OVERSOLD" (OS)

Traders tend to think in terms of absolutes. Somewhere in their career they have read in one or more trading books that when markets have risen to a high price the odds favor a decline, whether the decline is a correction in a bull market or the start of a bear market. To simplify their decision-making process, traders refer to such markets as being "overbought." On the other hand, markets that have declined for a fairly long time or that have had a steep decline in price are referred to as being "oversold." In both cases the label leads to an expectation or, at the very least, an implication that the current trend will soon be over. In both cases the assumption is not objective. It is more a function of trader perception, bias, and belief than it is a matter of fact.

In my estimation these terms are not only totally useless but as I indicated earlier, it is dangerous for the trader to think in such terms. A market will reverse its upward course once it has reached a level that no longer supports additional buying. A market will turn higher once it has declined to a level that attracts new buyers. This is the normal and historically valid process that dominates the behavior of and explains the price discovery process of all free markets.

If you have ever been to an auction then you know how this process works. A low price on a lot will tend, at a certain point, to start attracting bids. A high price will scare off additional bidders once it reaches a certain level. It is useless, in fact, counterproductive, to think of stock or commodity markets in any other terms. It has been clearly demonstrated to my satisfaction that the so-called random walk theory does not apply to the stock or futures markets or for that matter any free market. The random walk theory holds that prices are not predictable. It asserts that markets move randomly and that there are no real underlying trends.

My Stochastic POP Method (SP) is based on the overbought/oversold relationship, but in a fashion that is completely opposite from the traditionally accepted approaches. Before looking into the POP method, let's take a look at two of the traditional approaches to the SI application.

SI: THE 80/20 AND 75/25 METHOD

Let's take a look at a stochastic chart. Figure 12.1 shows an intra-day chart of E-Mini S&P with the SI. There are two SI lines, %K and %D. There are several methods that have been used with the SI as the timing indicator.

The 80/20 cross and the 75/25 cross are the most popular of SI applications. The rules are very simple. Depending upon which of the two extremes you choose, either 80/20 or 75/25, the following definitions of buy and sell signals are applicable.

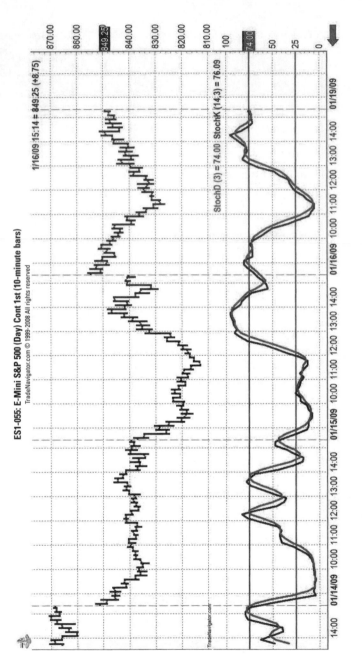

Figure 12.1. SI, 75%/25% boundaries, E-Mini futures, ten-minute bars.

Here's the Set-Up and Trigger:

- When SI percent K and/or D have risen above the 75 percent or 80 percent line and then declined below it, a sell signal is generated.
- When SI %K and/or %D have fallen below the 20 percent or 25 percent line and then risen above it, then a buy signal is generated.

Figures 12.2 and 12.3 illustrate the buy and sell conditions that are usually used with the SI. I have annotated the charts accordingly showing the traditional buy and sell signals.

As I have stated previously, many traders use the stochastic indicator as their preferred method of market timing or in conjunction with other timing methods as part of their decision-making process. My work with the stochastic indicator suggests that the traditional application used on its own may not be the best tool for traders. Remember, above all, that there is no upper limit for the price of any given market; however, there is a limit to the level that the stochastic indicator can reach on the upside: 100. By the same token, the limit to the level the stochastic indicator can reach on the downside is 0.

THE %K–%D CROSSOVER METHOD

George Lane offered a variety of methods for the use of his SI. His suggested application of the SI as an "overbought" or "oversold" indicator, which as I have already explained, has some serious limitations. George was not only a prolific technical analyst and researcher; he was also a brilliant teacher who

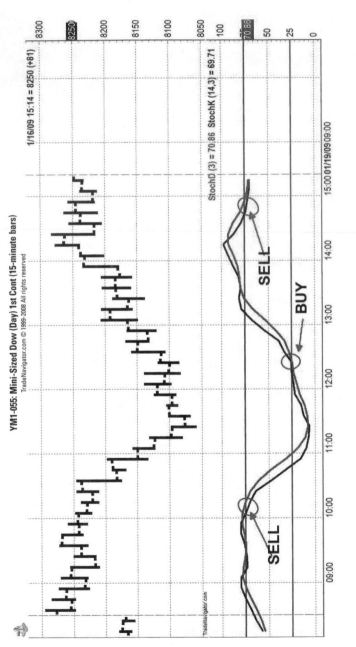

Figure 12.2. SI indicator, buy and sell signals, mini Dow futures, fifteen-minute bars.

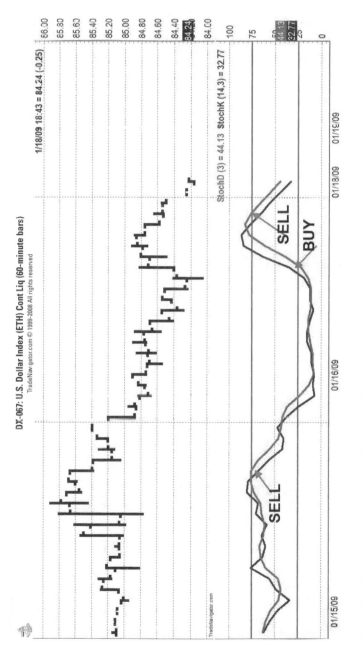

Figure 12.3. SI indicator, buy and sell signa s, U.S. dollar index, sixty-minute bars.

coached many traders. Another method that emerged from his teachings was the use of the SI as a timing trigger when the %K and %D lines crossed one another. This method has been used with varying degrees of success by traders. It is illustrated in chart form below. While I believe that there is some potential using this method the numerous false crossovers can be problematic.

The problem area shown in Figure 12.4 can be mitigated by changing the length of the %K and %D values. However, in so doing, all of the buy and sell points would be affected.

THE POP DAY TRADING METHOD

The POP Method approaches the stochastic indicator in a totally different way than the traditional method. In effect the POP Method generates a buy signal when the stochastic indicator is "overbought" and a sell signal when the stochastic indicator is "oversold." I realize that this sounds both strange and counterintuitive; however, I have observed that once the SI reaches a given high level or given low level, prices can more often than not continue in the given direction for a considerable amount of time and/or price distance.

The rules of application are simple and straightforward:

- Use a 9-period slow stochastic %K only with 3-bar smoothing.
- Use upper and lower boundaries of 30 percent and 70 percent.
- When %K crosses above 70 percent on the close of any bar, then buy on close of that bar.

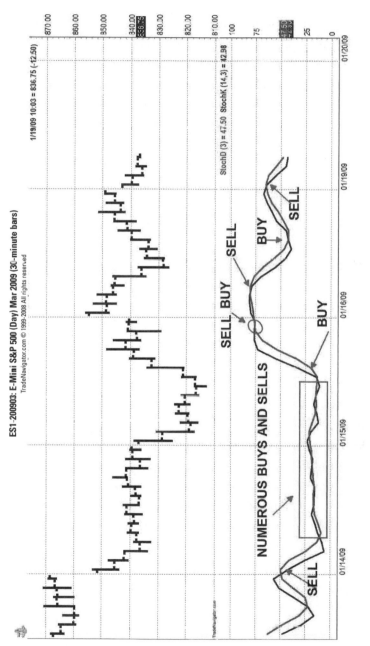

Figure 12.4. SI crossover signals, E-Mini S&P 5C0, thirty-minute bars.

- When %K crosses below 30 percent on the close of any bar then sell short on the close of that bar.
- Exit long when %K. crosses back below 70 percent.
- Exit short when %K crosses back above 30 percent.
- Or use a trailing stop loss once you have a profitable position.
- Trade *only* during the active portion of the contract in futures and only in actively traded stocks (i.e., average of 1 million shares daily).
- Most of the time the given market will move in the expected direction even if only briefly. Accordingly, day traders can exit for a small profit and then trail stops on remaining positions.
- Exit trades by the end of the day or on trailing stops or price spikes caused by news or overreactions due to other factors.

See the accompanying three charts for examples of this method. Note that this is *not* a trading system but rather a trading method. I say this because it is not totally mechanical. It requires some degree of judgment for exiting trades as well as close attention. Remember, as in all cases, the *big* money is made in the big move. This is why our goal is to hold positions as long as they are profitable or as long as profits are growing. I have previously advised you that one of the serious limitations of day trading is the necessity to exit positions at the end of the day. This, by definition, will limit profits.

Figures 12.5 through 12.8 illustrate the POP method:

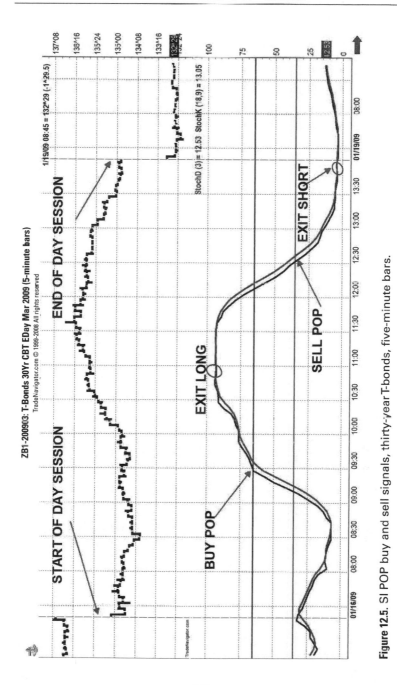

Figure 12.5. SI POP buy and sell signals, thirty-year T-bonds, five-minute bars.

217

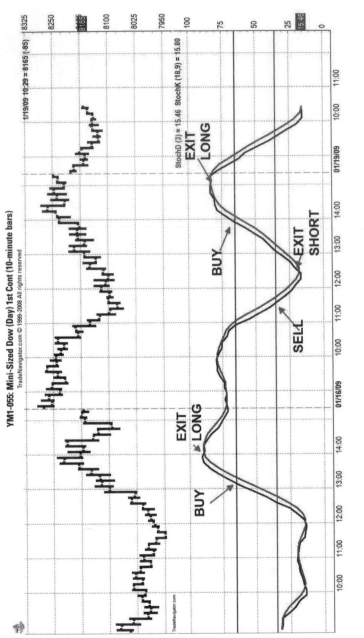

Figure 12.6. POP buy, sell, and exit signals, mini-Dow, ten-minute intervals.

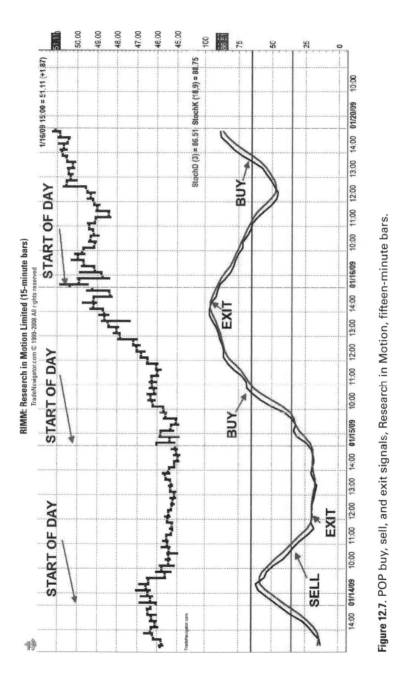

Figure 12.7. POP buy, sell, and exit signals, Research in Motion, fifteen-minute bars.

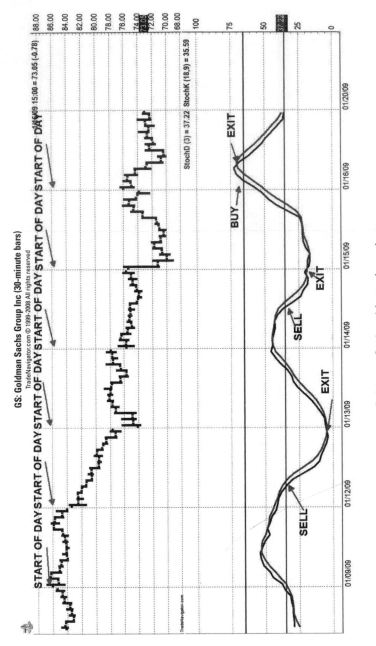

Figure 12.8. POP buy, sell, and exit signals, Goldman Sachs, thirty-minute bars.

Chapter **13**

The Trend Breakout Method

Perhaps the most effective and simple way to make money in the market is to trade with the trend. The trend is the path of least resistance. In a market that is trending higher, your odds of success as a buyer are higher than your odds of success as a seller. Conversely, in a down trending market your odds of success as a seller are higher than your odds of success as a buyer.

The concept is simple, but the application of this truism is not nearly as simple as one might imagine. There are several issues as follows:

1. How can we determine the trend?
2. How do we know when the trend has changed?
3. How can we determine where or when to enter a trade consistent with the trend?

In previous chapters I have given you several methods for determining when a trend begins and ends, and for buying at support in an up trend and selling at resistance in a down trend. While trading with the trend is a valid and effective method for day trading (assuming you are able to correctly determine the four points above), it is also possible to profit from what, for lack of a better descriptive term, I will call "trend breakouts" (TB). As in the case of trend trading, there are several prerequisites to the use of TBs. They are outlined below:

- How can we determine when a trend has "broken out" and started a new trend?
- Are there specific and objective methods we can use for entry and exit once a TB has developed?
- How can we manage the risk and maximize the profit in such trades provided we have objective methods and procedures for items 1–3 above?

WHAT IS A TREND BREAKOUT?

Although many traders use visual methods for determining the presence of a trend as well as trend changes, I find these methods sorely lacking in objectivity. Given that they are subject to interpretation they have no place in my work or in this book. In keeping with my goal of showing you methods with as close to 100 percent objectivity as possible, I will discuss the trend breakout method in terms of clear definitions methods and procedures.

Let us first begin with my definition of the term trend. As previously indicated, there are several ways in which we can define and determine a trend. When we use the moving average channel method with confirmation, a trend begins when there is a confirmed trigger on the indicators. When using the MACD, once the trend has been determined, the "swing trader" can make buy and sell decisions consistent with support or resistance. As an example, consider Figure 13.1.

Figure 13.1 shows how the day trader can buy at support once an up trend has started and how a profit can be taken once the market has moved to resistance. Conversely, the day trader can sell at resistance once a down trend has started and take profits when the market has dropped back to support (see Figure 13.2).

In the case of a new up trend, we establish a long position at predetermined support and we take profit at a predeter mined resistance (i.e., top of MA channel) whereas in a new down trend, we go short at the top of the channel (resistance) and we take profits at the bottom of the channel (support). In each case we trade with the trend.

As you well know, trends can and do change. They can change in direction, but within an existing trend there may be a new and strong movement in the upward direction. In a down trend, however, there may be a new and strong movement in the down direction. When a market "breaks out"—

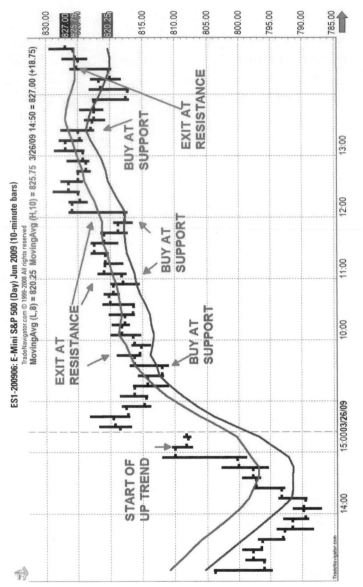

Figure 13.1. Buying at support and selling at resistance after new up trend signal.

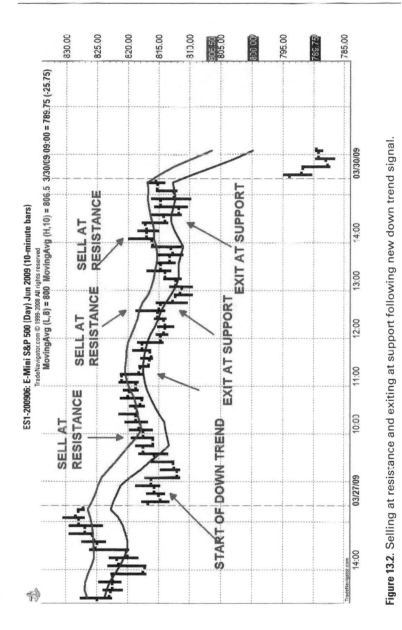

Figure 13.2. Selling at resistance and exiting at support following new down trend signal.

either in a new direction or in a strong direction within an existing trend—a trend breakout has occurred. The importance of a trend breakout is that it can often bring the short-term and day trader quick and reliable profits.

As a visual example of a trend breakout I offer the following two charts. Figure 13.3 shows a TB to the up side after a sideways trend whereas Figure 13.4 shows a trend breakout to the downside after a sideways movement.

In both cases the movement down was quick as well as large. The trader who had been "swing trading" within the MA channel (examples in Figures 13.1 and 13.2) would be stopped out of positions and would now be waiting for signals that a new trend has started. This could take some time, however, and in the interim a very profitable trading opportunity could be missed.

ENTER KELTNER

In the 1950s Chester Keltner developed a very effective strategy for spotting and trading trend breakouts. His channel method for trading futures used a moving average band, which, when penetrated in either direction, suggested that the given market was "breaking out." While there have been several variations on the original Keltner method, the concept is valid when applied in the correct fashion to stocks and commodities. I have taken some liberties with the original Keltner method as described below.

There is a considerable amount of information available about the Keltner method in a variety of technical trading books, articles, and Internet references. Note that my application of the method is based strictly on the concept and not on the method. I do not use a moving average as did Keltner;

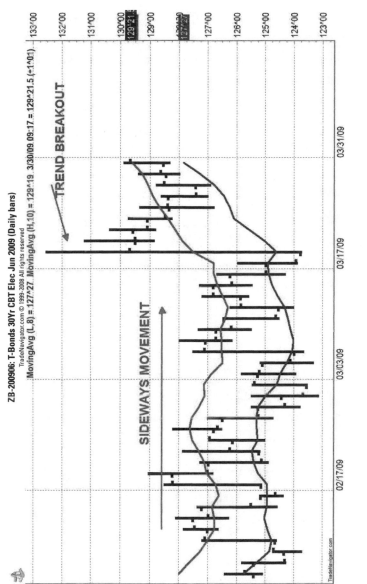

Figure 13.3. Trend breakout up after sideways movement.

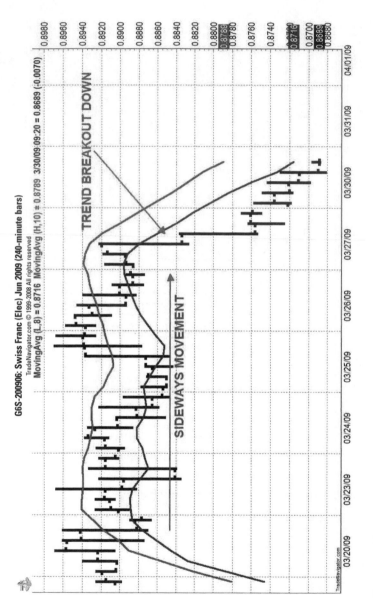

G6S-20090G: Swiss Franc (Elec) Jun 2009 (240-minute bars)
MovingAvg (L,8) = 0.8716   MovingAvg (H,10) = 0.8789   3/30/09:09:20 = 0.8689 (-0.0070)

TREND BREAKOUT DOWN

SIDEWAYS MOVEMENT

Figure 13.4. Trend breakout down after sideways movement.

rather I am merely using new highs or lows in prices over a given period of time.

SOME RULES AND EXAMPLES

Here are the general rules of application using my adaptation of the Keltner concept.

- Buy if price makes a new 16-period high.
- Sell if price makes a new 16-period low.
- Trail a stop loss or reverse your position on an opposite signal.

While the rules above seem simple enough, there are several other factors and variables to consider. Questions include:

- What number of price bars will trigger a buy or a sell?
- Should the number of bars for a sell signal and a buy signal be the same?
- What should be the first profit target?
- How should a stop loss be trailed?
- What length time chart should be used?

Prior to taking on these issues, let's take a look at some charts and explanations to illustrate the concept.

In the Figure 13.5, each of the up arrows indicates a new 16-period high in price. Each of the down arrows indicates a new 16-period low in price. As you can see, there are numerous consecutive arrows up in an up trend market. Each arrow up represents a trend breakout. An arrow in the opposite direction represents a trend breakout in the opposite direction.

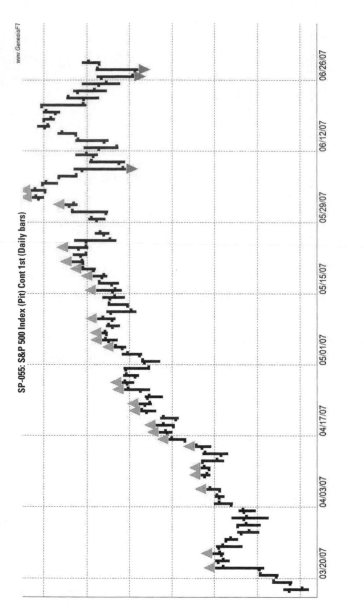

Figure 13.5. Canadian dollar futures (daily bars) showing new X day highs (arrows up).

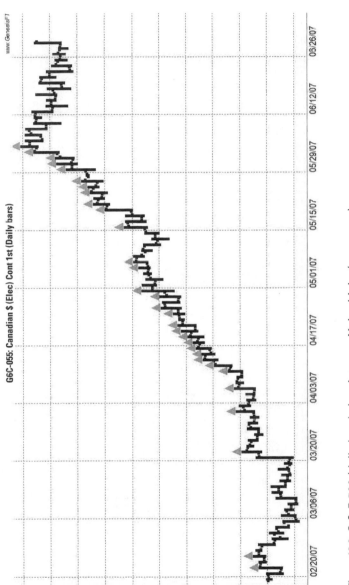

Figure 13.6. S & P 500 (daily bars) showing new X day highs (arrows up) and new X day lows (where X = the number of days).

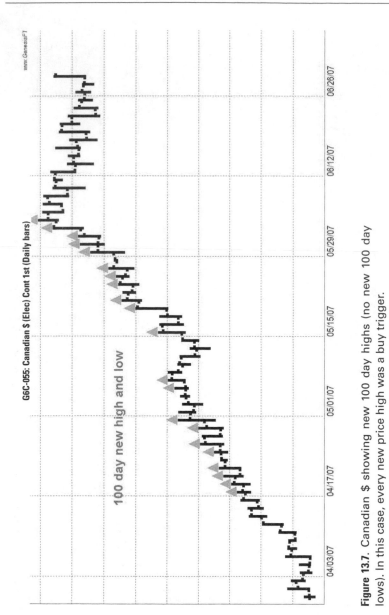

Figure 13.7. Canadian $ showing new 100 day highs (no new 100 day lows). In this case, every new price high was a buy trigger.

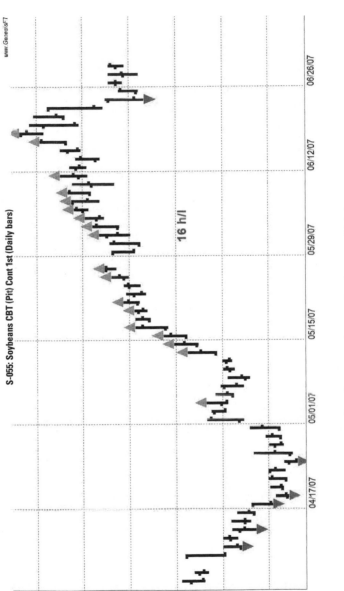

Figure 13.8. Soybeans daily chart showing new sixteen day lows and highs.

Following is an illustration of the signals within the framework of my STF model.

The buy Trigger in all of my examples is a new 16-period high, whereas the sell Trigger in all of my examples is a new 16-period low. The Set-Up in this case is the lowest low in the last sixteen bars or the highest high in the last sixteen bars. To enter an order you would do the following:

1. Note the higher high and the lowest low of the last sixteen price bars.
2. Place a buy stop one tick above the highest high.
3. Please a sell stop below the lowest low of the last sixteen price bars.

Note that in Figure 13.9 each of the new lows was a sell trigger and each of the new highs was a buy trigger. At the far right of the chart, an existing up trend was reversed to a new down trend by a new 16-bar low.

Whereas my previous charts illustrated this concept on daily charts, the following charts show the same method applied to intra-day charts. The Set-Up and Trigger are the same. Let's take a look at some charts before I discuss the Follow-Through for this method.

Note that in Figure 13.11 each of the down arrows at the left was a new sell trigger. A new up trend breakout developed at the first up arrow with each subsequent green arrow being a new buy trigger.

By now you should be clear as to what constitutes a Trigger and should have no difficulty in identifying it in Figure 13.12.

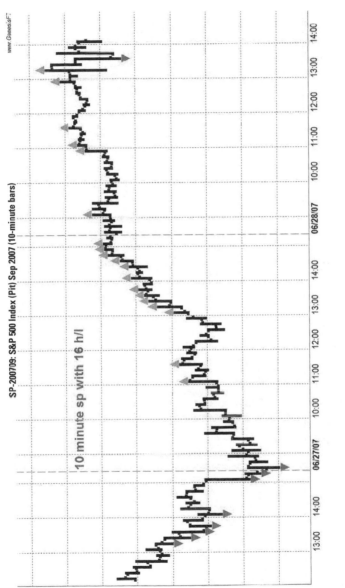

Figure 13.9. S & P 500 Index (ten-minute bars) showing the higher highs and lower lows indicator.

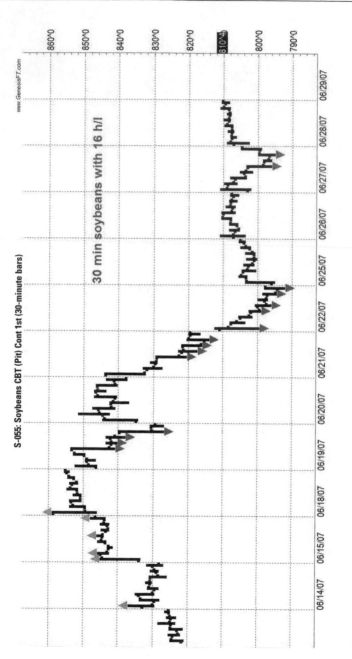

Figure 13.10. Soybeans (thirty-minute bars) with the higher highs and lower lows.

FILTERING

My experience with the higher highs and lower lows indicator suggests that using it alone as a day trading approach does not produce results that are as consistent or profitable as its use with a trend filter. The trend filter allows us to take only trades in the direction of the trend. This, in turn, reduces the number of trades but it increases the accuracy. The trend filter I suggest is a 14-period moving average of the 14-period momentum. When the 14-period momentum crosses above its 14-period moving average the trend is up and we can buy on new buy triggers. When the 14-period momentum crosses below its 14-period moving average the trend is down and we can only take the sell signals.

Figure 13.13 illustrates the method followed by a step-by-step description of the approach.

DESCRIPTION OF METHOD

Referring to Figure 13.13 above, here is a description of the method. When momentum is below its moving average, a down trend is in effect. A sell stop is placed to go short in the event that prices make a new 16-bar low. There are several possible exit strategies:

- Reverse your position on a new signal or if the relationship between momentum and its moving average changes.
- Exit part of your position after the fifth price bar is profitable and use a trailing stop strategy.
- Exit at end of day.

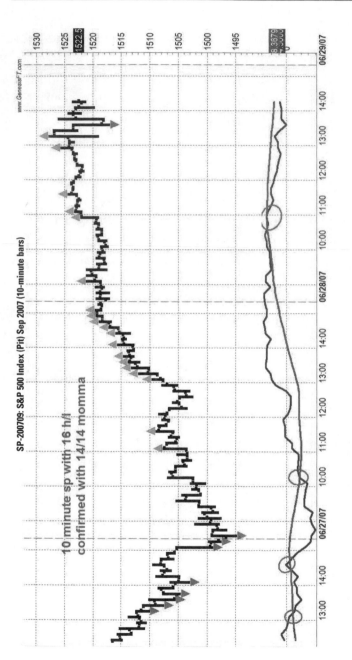

Figure 13.11. S&P 500 Index Sep (ten-minute bars) with momentum 14 and moving average 14 of momentum. Each of the circled areas represents a change in trend. Only signals in the direction of the trend are considered valid.

If you are an aggressive trader you can add to your position on each new signal.

If you are a conservative trader then you can raise trailing stops on every additional signal in the same direction.

Figure 13.14 provides another look at the method.

See figures 13.15 and 13.16 for several additional examples of this method of trading.

This chapter concludes Part II of this book and the discussion of technical trading methods. Part III carries on with practical tips for implementing trading methods and developing your own personal day trading system.

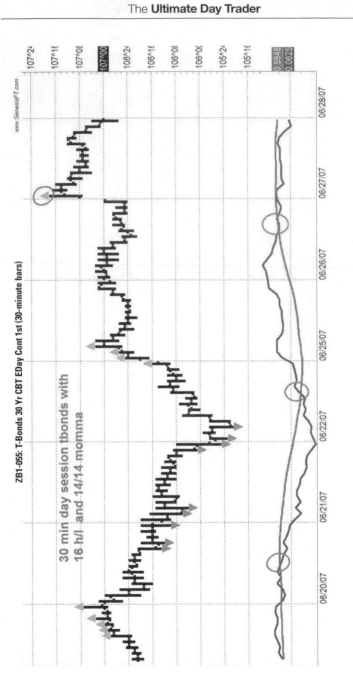

Figure 13.12. T Bonds 30 Year CBT (thirty-minute bars) with signals and momentum versus moving average confirmations.

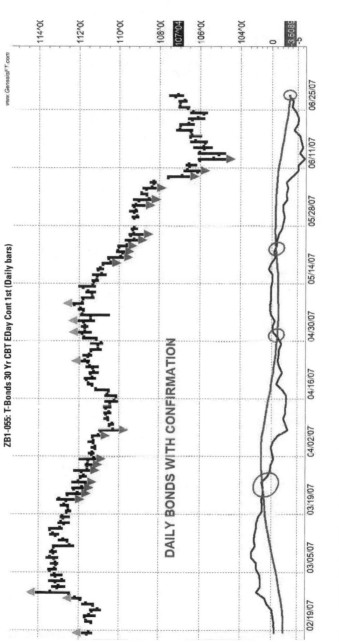

Figure 13.13. Daily T-Bonds (thirty-minute bars) with signal and confirmation using momentum and its moving average.

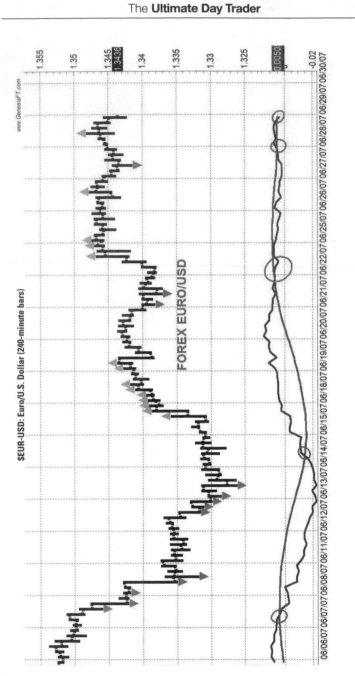

Figure 13.14. Forex Euro/USD Euro/US Dollar (240-minute bars) with signals and confirmation.

PART

AT THE END OF
THE DAY

Chapter **14**

Trading in a News-Driven Market

More than at any time in financial history, we live in

a news-driven market. Every day stocks, commodities,

and the FOREX markets make large moves in response

to news. In a time of economic crisis, these swings have

sometimes accounted for hundreds of points.

Whether the news is accurate or merely rumor is not an issue to day traders who thrive on news-driven markets. News that affects prices is not limited to such fundamentals as earnings, projections, mergers, proposed mergers, and/or government economic reports. Rumor, innuendo, indictments, brokerage house ratings upgrades and downgrades, reports in related markets, geo-political factors, as well as investor and trader sentiment are all affected by and in turn stimulate price moves. On many occasions the price moves that occur are very large because they stimulate emotional responses among traders.

INSIDER INFORMATION

Although the use of insider information in the financial markets often skirts legality, the fact is that it exists and that it is used by professional traders and investors who have access to the news. Insiders are aware of the news and act in advance of it. They establish positions before the news is made public, and when it results in a severe price reaction they exit their positions. If you believe that there is no insider trading simply because it is illegal then I have a bridge to sell you.

There are probably more ways to circumvent the laws against insider trading than there are laws against insider trading. Clearly the Securities and Exchange Commission, as well as the Commodity Futures Trading Commission and other regulatory agencies, have been only marginally effective in catching the culprits. Some of the largest frauds in history have been committed in the last several decades.

It is not my intent to make judgments about the morals or ethics of insider trading. I am a realist. I accept that it exists.

It is my task to show you how market reactions to news can be used to your advantage since most of us are not privy to insider information and we do not have the same advantage as those traders who use it.

ACTION AND REACTION

When news is released, markets react. If the news is anticipated then market reactions are relatively mild and, in some cases, virtually unnoticeable. When news is other than anticipated, then reactions in the markets are violent and lead to significant day trading opportunities. When news is unexpected, as in the case of a major world event, then the market reactions are severe. Very often, however, the initial market response to news is different than what the ultimate response may be. In other words, a negative news event may initially result in a large-priced decline. However, by the end of the trading day the market may have discounted the news and may end the day higher (at times much higher) than prices were when the news was initially announced.

Conversely, when a stock or commodity market opens sharply higher on positive news there is a tendency for prices to work lower and very often close lower than the opening price. At times the decline can be severe. Both situations are classic examples of the old market adage, "Buy the rumor and sell the news." Another epigram that has been frequently used to describe such situations is, "Buy on anticipation and sell on realization."

Let us not forget that markets and professional traders are forward thinking. We buy or sell on an expectation, and we exit when the expectation has become a reality. Even if we do not exit on the realization of an expectation, we often take profits on some of our positions and/or we trail stops to lock in profits once our expectations become realities.

MARKET TREND AND BIAS

Day-to-day price behavior in a market is often a function of underlying trends. While the longer-term trend, as assessed by monthly or weekly price charts, may not be a significant factor in finding profitable day trades, the daily price trend does, in my view, have an important role in biasing day-to-day activity. In fact, I have found that the underlying short-term trend as measured by daily price data can offer very reliable underpinnings for day trades using the opening and closing price relationship on any given day.

For the purposes of this chapter, I will only consider the large opening price rally or large opening price decline as measured from the closing of the previous day. It should be noted here that in markets that trade twenty-three-hour sessions such opening rallies or declines are usually not significant or worth considering. I prefer to use the "trade the news—fade the news" method primarily in stocks as opposed to futures.

THE METHOD

Now that you have some background regarding the logic and theory behind my approach here are some guidelines as to its implementation. Examples are included.

- First, select stocks that have opened sharply higher or sharply lower for the day as a result of news.

- A good metric for "sharply higher" or "sharply lower" is to select stocks that have opened lower or higher by at least 50 percent of the previous daily range. For example, assume that stock XYZ traded as high as $54 and as low as $50 yesterday. In this case you would look for an opening at least $2 below the low of the previous day (i.e., $48) or at least $2 above the high of the day (i.e., $56).

- This higher or lower opening should be motivated by news. The news can be based on earnings, upgrades, downgrades, politics, etc.

- Wait for fifteen minutes after the opening. This gives traders time to react to the news. Take no action during this time frame. The first fifteen minutes of trading is usually very volatile. Weak long holders are liquidating positions as stops are being hit. New sellers are entering the stock in anticipation of even lower prices. Buyers who already own the stock are entering the market since they see this as an opportunity to average their price on existing positions. New buyers who consider the stock to be a bargain are buying. Day traders are either buying or selling. And the opposite participation takes place when a strongly higher opening occurs based on news. We do not know, *a priori*, whether the bulls or the bears are correct. The stock will give us clues based on its behavior.

- After a sharply higher or lower opening as previously defined, the stock could go either way. Do not buy the stock simply because it seems to be cheap. Do not sell short because the stock seems to be expensive. Wait for the timing trigger to tell you what to do.

- Clearly, you will not always be right. I realize that you are well aware of this but I need to reiterate it so as to avoid creating unrealistic expectations.

- After the first fifteen minutes make note of the high and the low of the first fifteen-minute price bar.

- After a sharply *lower* opening based on news, *buy* the stock if it *ends* any fifteen-minute session above the high of the first fifteen-minute range after a sharply lower opening based on news. *Sell short* in the event of a fifteen-minute ending price below the low of the first fifteen-minute price range.

- In the event of a sharply *higher* opening, *sell short* in the stock if it *ends* any fifteen-minute session below the low of the first fifteen-minute range after the opening.

- Buy the stock in the event of a fifteen-minute ending price above the high of the first fifteen-minute price range.

- Risk a new low or high for the day.

- Exit on a price move in your favor either to a resistance level using some of the indicators presented in this book and/or exit by the end of the day and/or on a trailing stop once the trade is profitable.

LET'S LOOK AT A FEW EXAMPLES

As is often the case, examples in the form of a few charts tell the story.

NEWS ITEM: 17 December 2008. Newell Rubbermaid Inc. (NYSE:NWL) slashes its fourth-quarter forecasts for sales and earnings and announces global cost-cutting measures. The company cites a slowing in demand.

REACTION: NWL opens for trading $1.08 lower for the day. The previous daily range was 42 cents. The daily chart (Figure 14.1) shows the day in question.

Figure 14.2 shows the complete process on NWL (Newell Rubbermaid) on December 17, 2008, after it opened sharply lower due to a negative projection on sales and earnings.

The chart shows the day trading opportunity from trigger to exit on NWL for December 17, 2008, according to my "trade the news—fade the news" method. The Set-Up is the news and lower opening, and the "sell short" Trigger occurs after the third fifteen-minute bar closes lower then the range of the first bar. The Follow-Through is simply to cover at the end of the day.

Here's the second example:

NEWS ITEM: 14 January 2009 Bunge Ltd (NYSE:BG) opens sharply lower on bearish earnings estimate for 2008.

Figure 14.3 is the daily price chart of BG showing the decline.

Now look at Figure 14.4 to see the changes throughout the day.

Here's one more example:

NEWS ITEM: 8 January 2009 Billionaire investment fund manager Ron Burkle buys Whole Foods Market (NASDAQ:WFMI) stock.

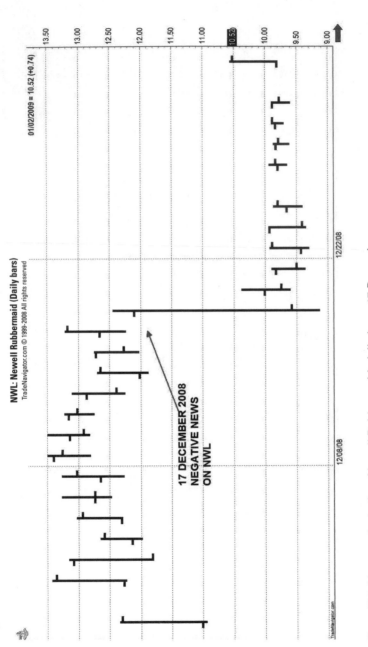

NWL: Newell Rubbermaid (Daily bars)
TradeNavigator.com © 1999-2008 All rights reserved

01/02/2009 = 10.52 (+0.74)

17 DECEMBER 2008
NEGATIVE NEWS
ON NWL

Figure 14.1. News and reaction, Newell Rubbermaid, daily bars. 17 December negative news on NWL creates a day trading opportunity.

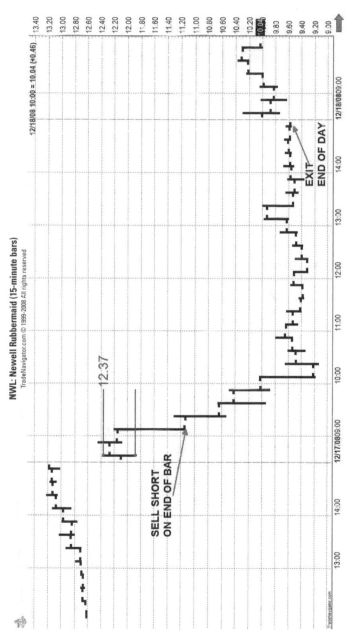

NWL: Newell Rubbermaid (15-minute bars)

Figure 14.2. News and reaction through the cay, Newell Rubbermaid, fifteen-minute bars.

253

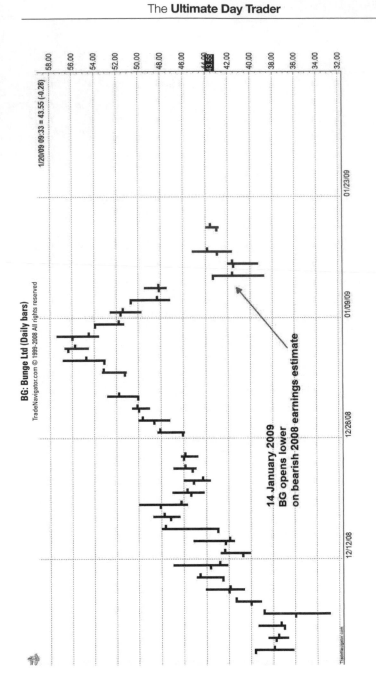

BG: Bunge Ltd (Daily bars)

1/20/09 09:33 = 43.55 (-0.28)

14 January 2009
BG opens lower
on bearish 2008 earnings estimate

Figure 14.3. News and reaction, Bunge Corporation, daily bars. The price of Bunge stock was hit by daily price decline on negative news on January 14, 2009.

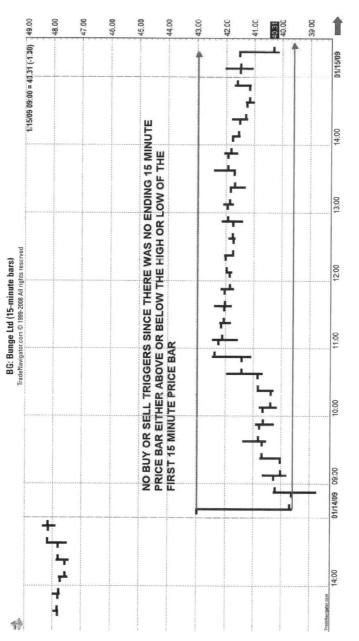

BG: Bunge Ltd (15-minute bars)

NO BUY OR SELL TRIGGERS SINCE THERE WAS NO ENDING 15 MINUTE PRICE BAR EITHER ABOVE OR BELOW THE HIGH OR LOW OF THE FIRST 15 MINUTE PRICE BAR

Figure 14.4. News and reaction through the day, Bunge Corporation, fifteen-minute bars.

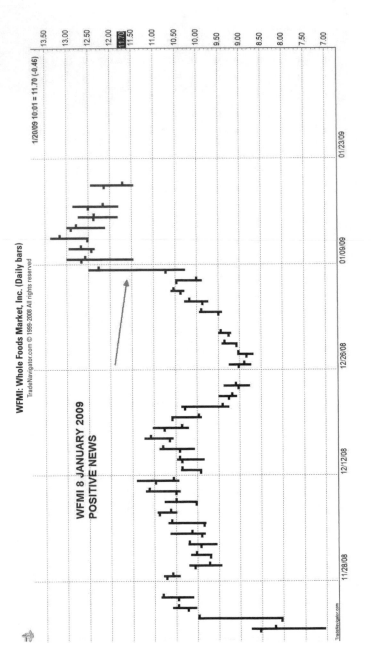

WFMI: Whole Foods Market, Inc. (Daily bars)

1/20/09 10:01 = 11.70 (-0.46)

WFMI 8 JANUARY 2009
POSITIVE NEWS

Figure 14.5. News and reaction, Whole Foods Market, daily bars.

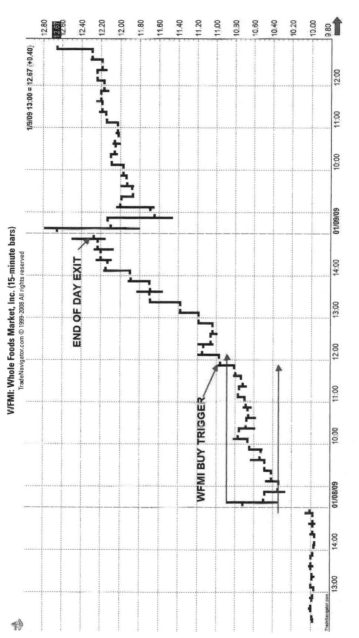

Figure 14.6. News and reaction through the day, Whole Foods Market, fifteen-minute bars.

Figure 14.5 is the daily chart of WFMI showing the price surge.

The shares surge higher on opening in reaction to this news on January 8, 2009. Now look at Figure 14.6 to see the reaction throughout the day.

In this case, the buy trigger finally occurs more than three hours after the opening.

This last example serves as a handy reminder that the trigger does not have to occur right away. The example before that (Figures 14.3 and 14.4), shows us that it doesn't have to happen at all. In the WFMI example, it's likely that a lot of market players, including market makers, sold into the initial rally. When that supply finally dried up, the market headed higher, with strength as some of those early sellers covered their shorts. This pattern occurs fairly frequently.

Chapter **15**

Exit Strategies

As I have indicated in previous chapters, the way in

which a day trader exits trades is often more important

than how she or he enters them. A highly accurate

entry strategy can be rendered useless if the exit

strategy being used does not maximize profits.

Many day traders are quite skilled and competent at entering positions. They have the ability, due to technical trading methods, experience, or a combination of the two, to time market entry precisely and with a high degree of accuracy. Their skills at exit methods, however, may well be sorely lacking. As a result, their inability to generate day trading profits proves even more frustrating than if their market entry methods were poor.

The purpose of this chapter is to discuss and illustrate a number of day trading exit techniques that will maximize your performance. You can also apply these profit maximizing strategies to other trading methods not covered here. Prior to giving you the details I want to remind you that your ultimate results will always be a function of several variables as described below. No matter how promising a method or strategy may be, there are limitations on performance that are above and beyond what any ideal situation can anticipate. Your profits will be limited by:

- **Follow-Through**—Your ability to Follow-Through on a trading plan using discipline combined with an effective sense of market judgment.
- **Limitations of pure day trading**—Trading in periods of time longer than a day trade allows more flexibility on exit strategies and increases profit potential. Day trades inherently limit this.
- **Ability to make subjective judgments**—Day trading involves a certain amount of skill and judgment that cannot be totally mechanical if it is to be successful.

- **Position size**—Your success will be either enhanced by or limited by the size of your position (i.e., the number of shares or contracts you trade).
- **Choice of markets**—Your success will be enhanced or limited by the specific markets or stocks you trade in. Simply stated, some stocks and commodities are more conducive to day trading profits than are others. Some guidelines regarding selection criteria are provided at the end of this chapter.

THE IMPORTANCE OF POSITION SIZE

The day trader has several advantages over the position (longer-term) trader. First and foremost among these is that the result of the trade(s) will be known by the end of the day. Feedback is almost immediate, and it enhances learning. In addition to receiving prompt feedback on results, the pure day trader is, by definition, forced to take profits or losses by the end of the day, giving a daily performance report on total success or failure.

Many traders, out of their inability to accept losses (and a lack of discipline) will carry losing trades beyond their prescribed exit point and/or beyond the end of the trading day. One of the exit strategies I will discuss below suggests carrying part of a winning position beyond the end of the day. This is acceptable because the trade is profitable. Importantly, *I do not, under any circumstances, advocate carrying a losing position to the next session.*

Let's look first at position size. The day trader who trades only one position (i.e., 100 shares in a stock or one contract in futures) is clearly at a disadvantage when it comes to exit strategies. The trade must be exited either at a stop loss, at a profit target, at a trailing stop, or at the end of the day. There is no ability to split the trade, that is, to allow profits to run while at the same time "taking some money off the table." In order to make profits consistently you will need to have large winning trades, unless you are highly accurate in your ability to repeatedly make small profits on small positions frequently. In my experience this is not easily or consistently achievable by most traders, unless they are on the trading floor where they are able to take advantage of very small price movements.

For most of us, the dream of being able to consistently reap small profits on small moves during the day is just that—a dream. I have seen many traders fail in their efforts to pursue this goal. Why? Because you may very well be able to achieve an amazing record of accuracy taking many small profits in a row—but a losing trade will eventually come, and it will often take all the previous profits or more.

As a result of this painful reality I urge you to consider trading in at least two units (i.e., lots of 100 shares of two futures contracts) so as to achieve more flexibility in an exit strategy that will allow you to carry winning positions. In so doing you will capture the largest profits, which will, in the end, make all the difference in your performance.

The "Pareto Principle" applies—at least 80 percent of your profits will be made on 20 percent of your trades. In order to make this market fact of life work for you, you will need to let part of your positions ride for maximum profits. There are several ways to do this. Here are a few general approaches.

EXIT STRATEGIES FOR SINGLE UNIT TRADING

If you're limited by circumstances or by choice to trade in single units—a single futures contract or 100-share unit of stock—your choices and profit potential may be limited. However, you can still succeed if you follow one or more of the strategies below. You will, though, be limited in how much profit you can take. Given this limitation you have several choices.

1. **Stick to trading methodology.** Take profits at a profit target that is generated by your trading methodology. **Do not** take profits based on "gut feel" or intuition. Use a specific method to arrive at your target, and use it consistently. The good news in taking profits at a profit target is that you will have banked the money. The bad news is that you will lose your ability to participate in a larger move. I have already stated why this is not preferable unless you can achieve and maintain very high accuracy while limiting losses to relatively small amounts.

2. **Look for a break-even target.** Determine a profit target that, if and when met, will be your cue to place a stop loss at break even. Break even is defined as your entry price. This will allow you to remove most of the risk from your trade while also allowing you to hold the position. If you are not stopped out, then you can exit at the end of the session. The good news is that you will have given yourself more opportunity to take the bigger profit. The bad news is that you may be stopped out repeatedly at break even. But is that really bad news? Think about it!

3. **Look for a second profit target.** You can implement strategy number two as noted above and use a trailing stop

procedure once a second profit target has been achieved. In other words, once the first profit target is achieved, enter the stop loss to keep the break-even intact and watch for the realization of a second profit target. If you use a second profit target, it should also be based on a consistent logic and/or method. This will avoid the placement of profit targets willy-nilly.

I recommend either strategy two or three as the preferred approach for one position (i.e., 100 shares of stock or one futures contract).

EXIT STRATEGIES FOR TWO-UNIT TRADING

Trading in two units gives you considerably more flexibility and will return larger profits in the long run. Here are your choices:

1. **Half-position closeout**. Take profits on one half of your position at a profit target that is generated by your trading methodology. **Do not** take profits based on "gut feel" or intuition. Use a specific method to arrive at your target and use it consistently. The good news in taking profits at a profit target is that you will have banked the money. The better news is that you will still have part of your position, which you can carry for a larger profit.
2. **Place a stop loss on the remainder of the position**. The profit target, if and when met, will be your cue to place a stop loss at break even on the remainder of the position. Break even is defined as your entry price. This will allow

you to remove most of the risk from your trade while allowing you to hold the second position. If you are not stopped out, then you can exit at the end of the session. The good news is that you will have given yourself more opportunity to take the bigger profit. The bad news is that you may be stopped out repeatedly at break even on this second position.

3. **Setup a second profit target on the second position.** You can implement strategy number two as noted above and use a trailing stop procedure once on the second position. You can also use a second profit target if you wish. If you use a second profit target please be sure that it is based on a consistent logic and/or method. The old rules still apply. Regardless of what you do, the position is closed out by the end of the session.

I recommend either strategy two or three as the preferred approach for two positions (i.e., 200 shares of stock or two futures contracts).

THE PREFERRED APPROACH

From experience, I prefer trading in units of three positions. Here's how it works:

1. **Take profits on first third.** Take profits on one third of your position at a profit target that is generated by your trading methodology. Again, **do not** take profits based on "gut feel" or intuition. Use a specific method to arrive at your target and use it consistently. Then, hold one third

of the remaining position with a break even stop. Hold one third of the position with a trailing stop that can be implemented immediately or when a second target is hit. The good news in taking profits at a profit target is that you will have banked part of the profit. The better news is that you will still have two-thirds of your position, which you can carry for a larger profit.

2. **Use second profit target**. You can implement strategy number one as noted above and use a break-even-based trailing stop procedure once on the second position. You can also use a second profit target if you wish. If you use a second profit target, please be sure that it is based on a consistent logic and/or method. Regardless of what you do, the second part of your position is closed out by the end of the session.

3. **Use third profit target**. You can exit another third of your position by the end of the session or you can exit the balance of the position by the end of the session. You can keep the profit target up and implement additional trailing stops. You can also implement a variety of trailing stop and/or profit target possibilities. As you can see, there is considerable flexibility. The key to the entire strategy is to get out of the danger zone with an initial break even stop loss and lock in at least some profit (i.e., initial stop loss) as soon as a profit target is hit, then build from there. I cannot emphasize this aspect strongly enough.

4. **Beyond day's end**. For those who seek adventure, one third of the position can be carried beyond the end of the session, but it should be noted that in so doing you will no longer be in a day trade, and you will no longer qualify

for day trade margin on that position. Furthermore, you will risk exposure of an opening price that may turn your profits into a loss.

I recommend either strategy two, three, or four as the preferred approach for three positions (i.e., 300 shares of stock or three futures contracts).

The suggestions noted above are applicable to virtually any of the methods I have discussed in this book. Next, let's take a look at some technical methods for trailing stops.

TRAILING STOP STRATEGIES

By "trailing stop" I mean the use of a buy stop or a sell stop that is designed to capture or lock in a percentage of the open profit on a position. By definition, a trailing stop (TS) is a stop that is changed every time the open profit in a trade reaches a new peak. It follows a few increments behind the price movement, up or down. Trailing stops on a profitable long position, for example, are always moving higher as the underlying market is moving in your favor. A trailing stop on a long position is never lowered. The opposite holds true for a trailing stop on a short position, which is never raised.

STRATEGY #1: TS USING A SIMPLE MOVING AVERAGE OF HIGH OR LOW PRICES

This is a very simple trailing stop method. Set the stop at the moving average of low prices for a long position or of the high prices for a short position. That allows the trade to fluctuate within a range but exits it if that range is breached. In the case of a long position that has reached its profit target, a stop loss of X units would be used. Many traders like to use a trailing stop of low prices as the stop. Figure 15.1 sets the trailing stop at the MA low for part of the position when the first profit target is reached.

The reverse would hold true in the case of a short position. In other words, you would use a 3 period MA of the highs. To broaden the range a little and if you want to give a market more leeway, you could raise the MA base to 5 periods or even more. The good news is that you will be giving the market more room, but the bad news is that you may give up more profit than you wanted to.

Parabolic Trailing Stop

A more dynamic way to trail a stop loss is to use the parabolic indicator. Developed by J. Welles Wilder, the parabolic indicator tends to more closely trail market moves. It takes into consideration price level as well as the upward or downward acceleration of prices. Figure 15.2 is a chart of the same E-Mini S&P 500 trade shown above but with a parabolic trailing stop.

Using the 8 Open/Close Indicator as a Stop

Yet another approach, one that gives the markets more leeway, is the 8 open versus 8 close indicator that I have developed. Here are the rules:

Use an 8 period simple MA of opening prices and an 8 period simple MA of closing prices. If you are long on a market, then the trailing stop is triggered when the 8-period MA of the close ends any bar below the 8-period MA of the open. The reverse holds true for a short position.

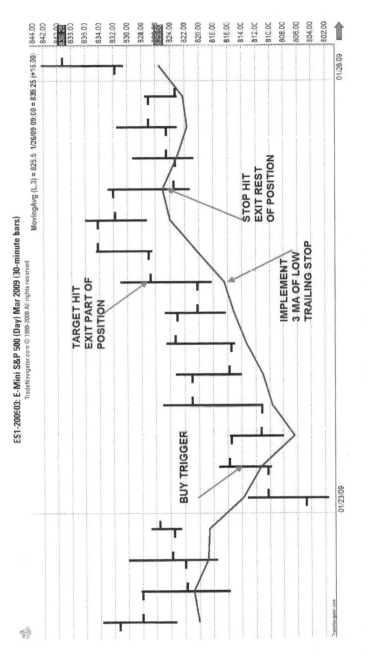

Figure 15.1. Moving average trailing stop, E-Mini S&P 500, thirty-minute bars.

269

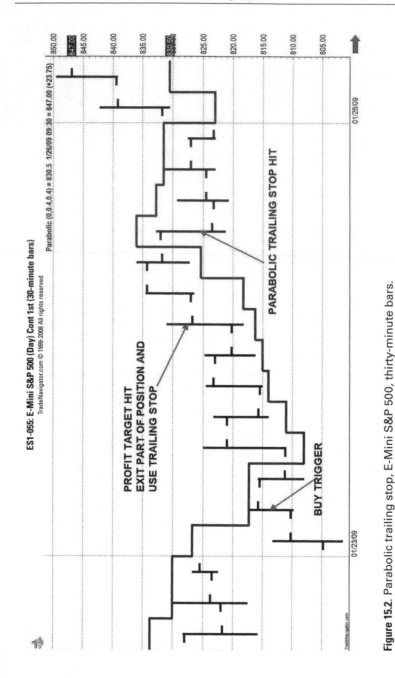

Figure 15.2. Parabolic trailing stop, E-Mini S&P 500, thirty-minute bars.

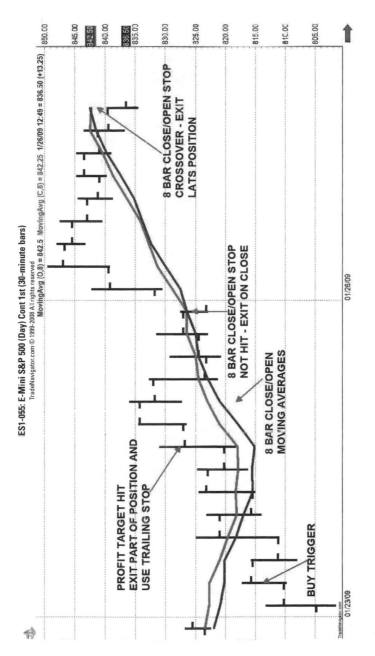

Figure 15.3. 8 Open/Close long trailing stop, E-Mini S&P 500, thirty-minute bars.

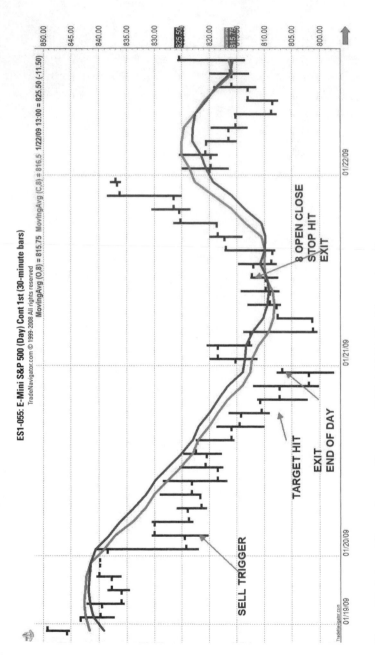

Figure 15.4. 8 Open/Close short trailing stop, E-Mini S&P 500, thirty-minute bars.

Figures 15.3 and 15.4 illustrate two examples of this approach. Note that the examples give a day trade more leeway, which, as noted earlier, can work for you or against you. I recommend this approach in cases where you want to carry part of your position to the next trading session.

Over time and with experience you'll determine your own best exit strategies, which may vary according to your profit objectives, risk tolerance, and the markets you trade. From here, we move into still more general principles—I call them "pragmatics"—of day trading.

Chapter **16**

The Pragmatics of Day Trading

Now that we have examined a number of day

trading methods and procedures as well as Follow-

Through methods, it's time to learn how to put all the

information together into a meaningful whole. For the

day trader who employs only one method, the details

in this chapter will not be as important. However, I

hasten to add that I do not recommend the "one trick

pony" approach to day trading.

The simple fact of the matter is that not all market moves are created equal, and one method or system will not serve you as well as a diversified approach in methods as well as markets. This chapter will focus on three aspects of day trading that will, if effectively implemented, facilitate your success as well as the consistency of your results. These three areas of concern are:

- Diversification of methods and systems
- Procedures for implementation
- Trade management

After covering these areas, we will talk more about the trading tools themselves, i.e., the hardware and software that make it all work.

DIVERSIFICATION OF METHODS AND SYSTEMS

Harry Markovitz, in his Nobel Prize-winning work, stressed the importance of diversification of assets in the equities and commodities markets. In short, he found that trading a balanced portfolio of stocks and futures gave the best results in terms of consistency and in terms of "smooth" performance. Trading a non-duplicated and non-correlated basket of stocks and futures was the best overall strategy in terms of performance.

The application of this approach is simple enough for the day trader. Rather than day trading four stocks and perhaps one futures market, all five markets in the energy sector, the best result would be achieved by trading stocks in four completely unrelated stocks and one unrelated futures market. A good mix could be a gold mining stock, a technology stock, a financial stock, and a retail stock combined with a day trade in soybean futures.

Although it's unlikely I'll win a Nobel Prize for the following, the fact is that there are, in my view, at least two additional levels of diversification. These are:

- Diversification across trading methods
- Diversification across time frames

Diversification across Trading Methods

The day trader who trades only one method may very well become an expert at that method. However, the behavior of a given stock or commodity market does not always fit the method because the fundamentals that move that market can be radically different at different times in the economic and business cycles.

One tool does not fit all types of market moves. Some tools may be useful in taking small parts out of an existing trend while other tools may be more suited to picking tops and/or bottoms. I therefore suggest that you keep at least three different day trading tools in your toolbox of methods and systems. I have given you several different alternatives in this book. I urge you not to restrict yourself to just one method.

Naturally this raises the questions as to what should be done in the event of contradictory signals. The answer is simple: the method that triggers first is the method that you will use. The follow-up method you will use is the method that is specific to the strategy that got you into the trade. It's really quite simple.

DIVERSIFICATION ACROSS TIME FRAMES

Although you may want to be a day trader and nothing else, I suggest that this is a short-sighted goal. In order to take advantage of opportunities in all time frames, you need to give yourself an opportunity to participate in them. Hence, I suggest that you participate in the markets as an investor as well as a day trader. As an investor there are some positions you will want to hold for the intermediate or long term. You don't want to trade everything, because you can't afford to lose everything. Moreover, even a day trader will retire at some point. Planning for your retirement with some longer-term investments is highly recommended.

POSITION SIZE

In the last chapter, we covered position size and the flexibility of trading multiple units instead of a single contract or 100-share lot. Here are some more suggestions, including some thoughts on when to increase position size:

- **Trade in units of three if possible**—By this I mean 300 shares of a stock or 3 contracts of a commodity—as covered in the last chapter.
- **When to ramp up size**—As a general rule you can increase the size of your positions once you have generated at least 50 percent profit in your account.
- **Use the suggested Follow-Through procedure**—Apply this to each method you use.
- **Pay attention to the "danger zone" concept**—I discussed this previously; it is very important. Make cer-

tain that once you are out of the danger zone, then you Follow-Through the remainder of your position(s) with profit maximizing strategies.

- **Pay attention to risk**—Make decisions as to position size based on the anticipated risk as opposed to the anticipated profit.

PROFIT MAXIMIZING STRATEGIES USING MONEY MANAGEMENT PROGRAMS

In addition to the profit maximizing strategies noted above there are other ways to increase trading profits. Once you have established your methods and procedures you can investigate these approaches. By evaluating the trading performance, account size, and your individual trades, these programs can suggest the number of shares of contracts to trade each time. As an example, consider the short-term trading system results for a method that trades the European currency futures. Here is the system performance record with slippage and commissions deducted trading one contact per trade.

SUMMARY—ALL TRADES REPORT

Overall			
Total Net Profit	$131,550	Profit Factor ($Wins/$Losses)	3.06
Total Trades	155	Winning Percentage	74.2%
Average Trade	$849	Payout Ratio (Avg Win/Loss)	1.06

Overall (con't)			
Avg # of Bars in Trade	7.37	Z-Score (W/L Predictability)	−0.6
Avg # of Trades per Year	21.9	Percent in the Market	55.2%
Max Closed-out Drawdown	−$8,938	Max Intra-day Drawdown	−$10,075
Open Equity	−$2,763		
Current Streak	1 Loss		

Winning Trades		Losing Trades	
Total Winners	115	Total Losers	40
Gross Profit	$195,488	Gross Loss	−$63,938
Average Win	$1,700	Average Loss	−$1,598
Largest Win	$10,438	Largest Loss	−$3,700
Largest Drawdown in Win	−$3,700	Largest Peak in Loss	$1,500
Avg Drawdown in Win	−$699	Avg Peak in Loss	$593
Avg Run Up in Win	$3,224	Avg Run Up in Loss	$593
Avg Run Down in Win	−$699	Avg Run Down in Loss	−$2,141
Most Consec Wins	15	Most Consec Losses	4

Winning Trades (con't)		Losing Trades (con't)	
Avg # of Consec Wins	4.11	Avg # of Consec Losses	1.38
Avg # of Bars in Wins	8.24	Avg # of Bars in Losses	4.88

Figure 16.1. All trades report, Euro currency futures, single contract per trade.

Despite the fact that only one contract was traded at a time, the record shows a healthy profit over a seven-year period of relatively less active trading; each year averaged about twenty-two trades. The growth in positive equity is further illustrated by the equity curve, showing the cumulative gain, in the next figure.

The historical performance chart of this method, again trading one contract per signal with slippage and commission deducted is shown in Figure 16.2.

If you use the same system as the method of generating trades but trade more than one futures contract, based on a specific position management formula outlined above and in Chapter 15, you will be able to generate considerably more profit. The equity curve chart below shows the performance of the one-contract approach (as above) with a second line depicting a simple money management approach, as illustrated in Figure 16.3.

There are a number of approaches to profit management. They are based on a variety of factors that take a number of variables into account. Before you implement such strategies, make certain that your day trading is profitable and that all of your procedures are in order. Comparisons such as the one above will not become realities if you are not diligently managing your risks.

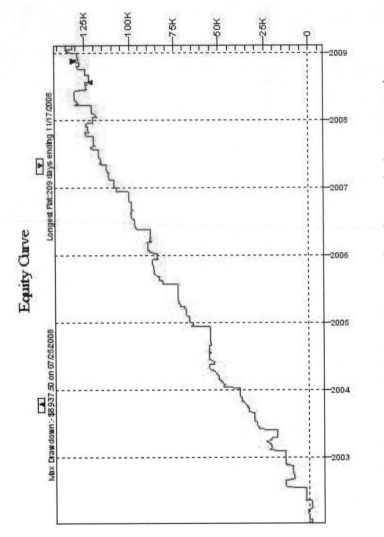

Figure 16.2. Equity curve, cumulative performance, Euro futures, single contract trades.

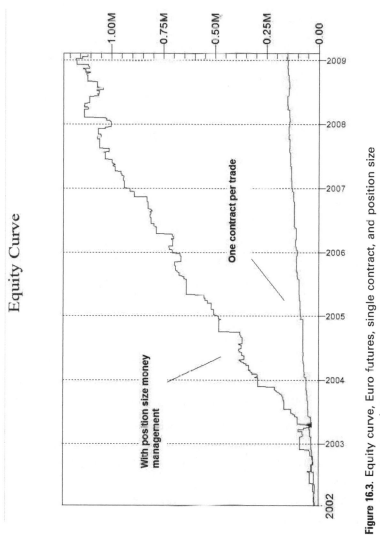

Figure 16.3. Equity curve, Euro futures, single contract, and position size management approaches.

283

INFORMATION SOURCES

Another obvious aspect of successful day trading is the use of reliable and accurate data sources. Successful day trading depends in part on prompt, reliable, and timely price information. If the analytical program you are using is too slow to process data or if it displays numerous data errors, then your results will be severely limited. Speed of data delivery is of the utmost importance if your trading signals are to be generated on a timely basis.

As you know, time is of the essence in entering and exiting day trades. Some software programs are slow in generating signals and/or in updating your indicators. Before you pay good money for any trading software, "test drive" the program to see how quickly your data is updated.

DATA LINE CONNECTIVITY

The faster you get your data delivered to you, the more promptly you can enter and exit trades. I strongly suggest getting the fastest broadband Internet connection you can afford. Seconds count when making day trades. Cable-provided Internet connections are the fastest and best outside of an expensive business T1 line. Today's 5 or 10 megabit DSL is good, although you can do a lot of trading on slower services. It's a good idea to have a second, or backup, connection path in case the first one goes down. Some traders insist on day trading with slow connections or dial up connections in order to save a few dollars. I strongly advise you not to use a slow connection. In fact, get the fastest connection you can afford.

ELECTRONIC TRADING ACCOUNT PLATFORM

In my own trading I have observed that some electronic order entry platforms and brokers are much faster than others. Without mentioning names, one of the brokerage firms I used for online trading was dreadfully slow. The program also froze up several times a week. In a number of cases this poor performance cost me money. This is unacceptable. You need to use a broker and a platform that gives you the fastest response times available. Furthermore, your order executions need to be reported back to you promptly so that you will know exactly where you stand. This is essential for profitable trading!

Do your research before you open an account. Get answers. Talk to other traders or test drive the platform. Don't be afraid to ask questions. In addition, make certain that there is a backup procedure and account for placing orders in the event that your connection fails or if the electronic order entry platform fails to function. As a day trader you need to make certain that you can enter and exit positions promptly and on a timely basis; a bad trade that can't be properly closed out because of a system glitch can cost you a pile of money.

EASE OF USE

I have found some electronic trading platforms to be very confusing. You need a platform that is simple and clear while also being effective and flexible. I will not name names here, but there are significant differences. Ask for a demonstration of the platform before you open an account with any brokerage firm. Many firms have online demonstrations of their platforms. Take advantage of these demonstrations and/or practice accounts.

COST OF COMMISSIONS AND FEES

As an active day trader, one of your largest and ongoing costs will be commissions. The natural tendency is to go with the brokerage firm that will give you the lowest commissions. While this may seem apparent, it is not necessarily correct. A cheap commission will not serve you well if service is slow, if the trading platform is flawed or prone to disruptions in service, or if the price executions on the market orders are habitually bad. Take your time to evaluate commissions in light of other features that are offered by the brokerage firm.

ORDER TYPES

Recently some online brokers have added a variety of order types to their platforms. The most important of these, explained in previous chapters, is the "trailing stop" feature. I find this tool to be very useful when you are riding a position for which you wish to lock in a profit on a trailing stop loss basis. The trailing stop has been explained previously in Chapter 15. You'll save considerable time if the computer can automatically trail a stop for you. As your position makes new profit highs in your favor, the computer will change your trailing stops, which will in turn allow you to give more attention to other trades and to new possible trades. This feature is a fantastic addition to the day trader's repertoire. Look for an online broker that provides this time saving order type. Choose the online broker that will give you the most order type features.

ALERTS AND OTHER TOOLS

In addition to the trailing stop tool, there are other time-saving and opportunity-finding tools. Among these are alerts that will watch the markets for you and advise you when certain conditions and/or criteria have been met. They will thereby alert you to possible trading opportunities. Alerts are excellent time savers. Your trading software and/or your online account should give you the ability to program a wide variety of alerts based on indicators and prices. These are also very important, pragmatic tools for success.

FILTERS AND CRITERIA

As it turns out, finding the trading opportunity often is the hardest part. Software technology also provides us with the ability to search through thousands of stocks and commodities worldwide for specific criteria. These filters and screeners can alert you to developing opportunities within seconds of their occurrence. A filter allows you to scan a large number of selected markets for specific criteria at any time. These filters or criteria have been predetermined and can be searched for at any time. As an example, every day after my data has been downloaded I look for markets with certain criteria. These have been programmed into the computer and are designed to show me markets that meet my specific criteria. Here, for example, in figures 16.4 and 16.5, are sample lists of my filters and filtering criteria:

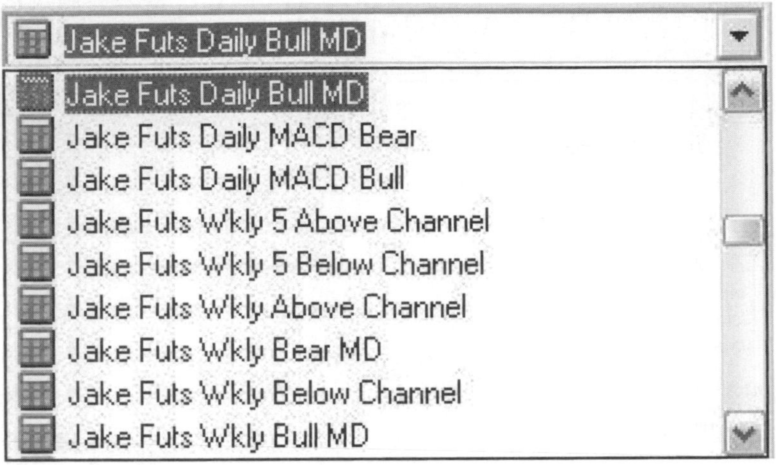

Figure 16.4. Futures trade filter settings.

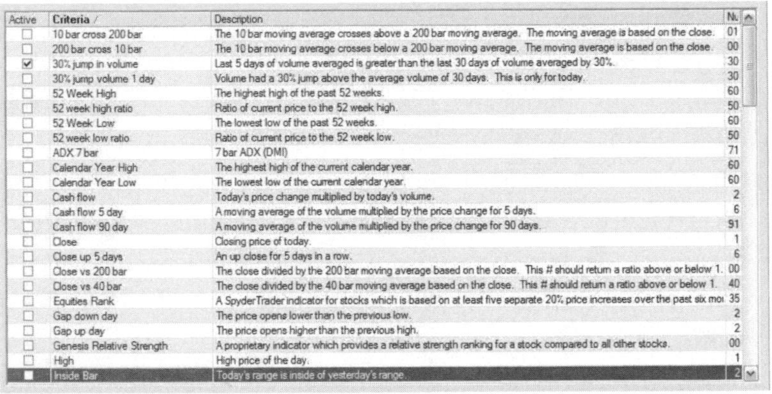

Active	Criteria /	Description	Nu
☐	10 bar cross 200 bar	The 10 bar moving average crosses above a 200 bar moving average. The moving average is based on the close.	01
☐	200 bar cross 10 bar	The 10 bar moving average crosses below a 200 bar moving average. The moving average is based on the close.	00
☑	30% jump in volume	Last 5 days of volume averaged is greater than the last 30 days of volume averaged by 30%.	30
☐	30% jump volume 1 day	Volume had a 30% jump above the average volume of 30 days. This is only for today.	30
☐	52 Week High	The highest high of the past 52 weeks.	60
☐	52 week high ratio	Ratio of current price to the 52 week high.	50
☐	52 Week Low	The lowest low of the past 52 weeks.	60
☐	52 week low ratio	Ratio of current price to the 52 week low.	50
☐	ADX 7 bar	7 bar ADX (DMI)	71
☐	Calendar Year High	The highest high of the current calendar year.	60
☐	Calendar Year Low	The lowest low of the current calendar year.	60
☐	Cash flow	Today's price change multiplied by today's volume.	2
☐	Cash flow 5 day	A moving average of the volume multiplied by the price change for 5 days.	6
☐	Cash flow 90 day	A moving average of the volume multiplied by the price change for 90 days.	91
☐	Close	Closing price of today.	1
☐	Close up 5 days	An up close for 5 days in a row.	6
☐	Close vs 200 bar	The close divided by the 200 bar moving average based on the close. This # should return a ratio above or below 1.	00
☐	Close vs 40 bar	The close divided by the 40 bar moving average based on the close. This # should return a ratio above or below 1.	40
☐	Equities Rank	A SpyderTrader indicator for stocks which is based on at least five separate 20% price increases over the past six mo	35
☐	Gap down day	The price opens lower than the previous low.	2
☐	Gap up day	The price opens higher than the previous high.	2
☐	Genesis Relative Strength	A proprietary indicator which provides a relative strength ranking for a stock compared to all other stocks.	00
☐	High	High price of the day.	1
☐	Inside Bar	Today's range is inside of yesterday's range.	2

Figure 16.5. Filter criteria sample.

SCREENERS

Screeners are also a wonderful tool. Rather than simply analyzing markets for the same criteria over and over, screeners allow you to ask certain questions and to get specific

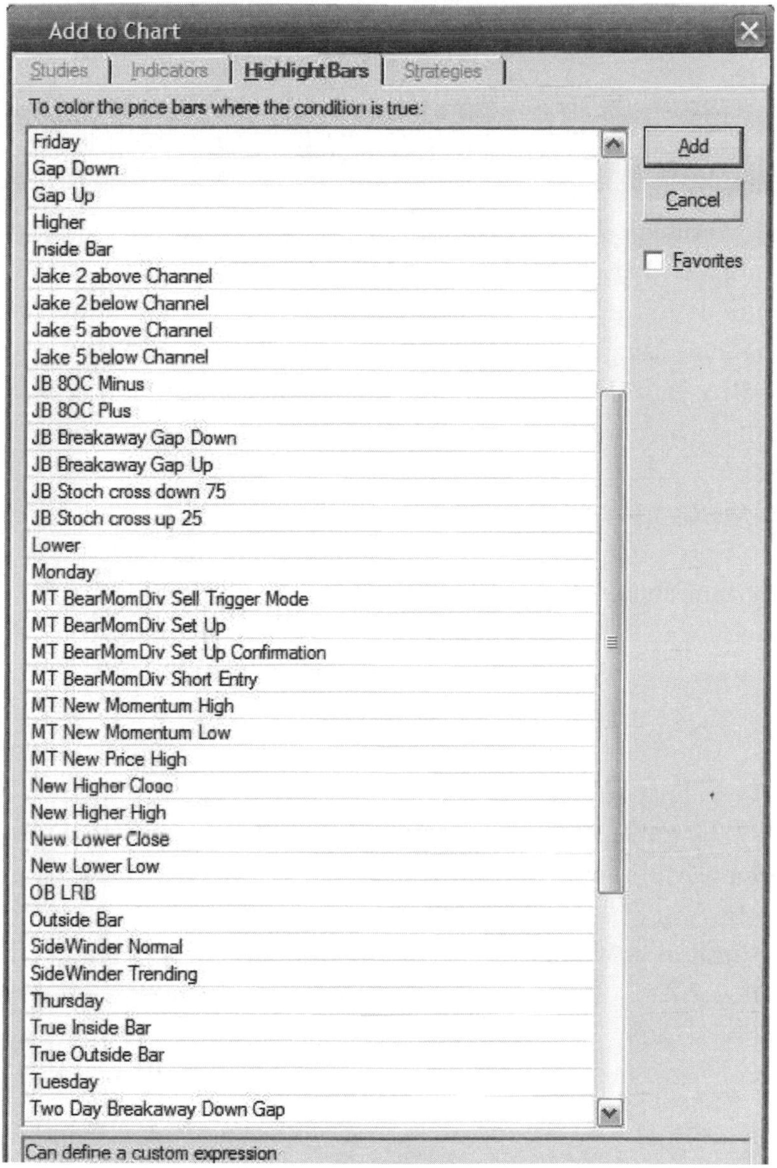

Figure 16.6. Highlight Bar criteria example.

answers very quickly. As an example you might want to know the following:

Show me all stocks between $5 per share and $35 per share that have shown a 300 percent increase in daily number of shares traded from the day before.

In practice you can screen for this set and a host of other variables that might give you clues as to developing day trades. The software also allows me to define my own criteria for screens, using very simple programming language. This is not only a valuable tool for finding trades, but it is also valuable for researching new methods.

HIGHLIGHT BARS STUDIES

Your trading software should also allow you to highlight certain characteristics on a chart. Say, for example, that you wanted to color all reversal bars in red; you could do so by either selecting or writing an instruction for this feature. Here, for example, in Figure 16.6, are some of the highlight bar studies that can be run on the Genesis™ software that I use in my trading.

You can see the power and flexibility inherent in these tools. But as with any tool, they can be dangerous if used improperly. It will be worth the time to study and experiment with all the tools in the trading toolbox. It's all part of pragmatic thought about trading. Hopefully the considerations noted in this chapter will go a long way in facilitating your success as a day trader.

Chapter **17**

Putting It All Together

It's one thing to have solid trading methods and indicators. It is an entirely different thing to use them effectively. In this book I have given you a number of trading methods and strategies. I have attempted to be as specific as possible in doing so. In addition to the use of effective systems and methods, a significant key to a day trader's success is organization.

Being organized can either enhance performance or inhibit performance. The active day trader must not only implement profitable strategies consistently but must also avoid many of the costly errors that inhibit profits or, in the worst case scenario, result in losses. While the problem may be obvious, the solutions may not be as clear. While the solutions may seem dull and mechanical, they are necessary if success as a day trader is to be achieved. This chapter will give you some guidelines as to how you can implement, manage, and maximize the strategies discussed in this book. It should be noted that these strategies can be implemented with any trading approach since they are basic, indeed essential, elements of profitable trading.

DAY TRADING IS A BUSINESS

It is imperative that you view your day trading activities as a business. To simply day trade as a lark, as an adventure, as "a shot," or as "a gamble" is unacceptable. This approach will not take you where you want to go. How you view your day trading is a pretty accurate predictor of how you will perform as a day trader. If you view your day trading purely as a challenge or as a something you need to do in order to prove something to yourself or others, then you are not likely to succeed. All too often I have heard traders say, "I think I'll buy that stock. I like what I hear in the news today. If it's profitable at the end of the day I'll get out, but if it's a losing trade I'll keep it as an investment because it's a good company."

This sort of mixed logic is wrong. The vocabulary is wrong. The psychology is wrong. And the end result is likely to be wrong.

Day trading is a business and must be run as such. By this I mean that you need to keep track of the following facts every day before you trade, after you trade, and while you trade:

Your cost of doing business. This includes commissions and fees, margin costs if you day trade in a margin account, as well as the cost of your information services and trading software. While these are fixed costs—at least to some extent—you need to know the monthly or even daily cost of doing business. If you day trade from home or from your office then the cost of your office space is yet another factor. Determine your average or typical cost of doing business. Note also that some of these costs, perhaps all of them may be deductible from your taxes, depending on whether trading is your primary occupation or source of income. Consult a tax professional for information on this aspect of trading.

Your business model. Every business needs a model. You need to have, develop, or acquire a business model for your trading venture. The model I have presented in this book is Set-Up, Trigger, and Follow-Through. The underlying aspects of this model are the trading methods, which need to be clearly delineated and implemented according to the rules. Later in this chapter I will give you some guidelines as to how this can be achieved.

Organization and structure. Every business needs an organizational structure within which day-to-day operations are performed. By this I mean that as a day trader you need to have a precise schedule. Will you be working every trading day? I say yes, you need to. Will you be working specific hours? I say yes, you need to. You cannot operate success-fully as a day trader by keeping inconsistent hours or work-ing days. If you have trading systems and methods then you need to apply them every day lest you miss opportunities. Within this structure you must also have a set of clear pro-cedures by which you implement your trades. Which meth-ods will you use? When will you use them? Will you make random decisions about what method or methods to use? Do you have all of your trading rules written down and eas-ily accessible?

Business processes implementation. Whether you use the methods suggested herein or others, you need to have clear and concise procedures for implementing them. What time of day will you place orders? Will you place all orders with one broker or in one account? Do you have a method of quality control? By this I mean are you certain you are not duplicating orders? Have you planned your day? Do your trades need to be placed at specific times? How are you finding your setups and triggers? Are you using technol-ogy to reduce the possibility of errors and/or to make your work more efficient?

Record-keeping. This is of the utmost importance. If your record-keeping is erratic or incomplete, then you will not only make errors of omission but you may also make errors in placing orders. Fortunately your online account has features to help you do this. My experience, however, has taught me that online account tracking is, in many cases, not sufficient. All too often you do not know where you stand in your day trades. If you are only day trading one or two stocks or futures markets, then you can easily handle all positions and orders mentally or with brief written or computer filed notes. On the other hand, if you trade multiple positions with multiple share lots or contracts, the issue becomes more complicated. You will either need to use a professionally designed program or create one of your own. Some of the more advanced trading and charting programs have the ability to do this.

EFFICIENCY

As an active day trader it behooves you to use computer technology to your advantage. Every second you can save by relegating rote tasks to the computer is a second you can devote to your trading and/or research. To this end I strongly recommend the use of scans and filters to find your trading opportunities. This is especially important in stock trading due to the sheer number of potential opportunities available to you on any given day.

Consider the following situation. At the start of the trading day I want to find all stocks that have given a particular setup or trigger after the first thirty minutes of trading. I have several choices:

- **I can keep a predetermined list of stocks that I want to trade**. I can then go to the chart and indicators of each stock and commodity and look for the triggers or setups manually. This takes time. As a day trader, time lost = opportunities lost. This is unacceptable.

- **I can allow the computer to scan all stocks and commodities for me**. This will take much less time and it will cover a huge universe of potential trades.
- **I can refine scans**. Once the computer has performed the scans I can refine the scans using the computer.
- **I can set up additional passes**. Once I have refined the scans to a manageable number of opportunities, I can either let the computer make a further parse of the data, or I can do a manual selection.

All of the above can be readily achieved in any of the professional charting and trading packages. Here is an example of what I mean. Figure 17.1 shows a scan that I ran on a particular trading setup. The scan shows all stocks that meet my criteria at the start of trading on a given day. By clicking on any of the symbols I can bring up the chart of that stock and determine my course of action.

Note that there are 183 possible opportunities on this list. By going back to the filter and selecting more precise criteria I can narrow down the list as shown in Figure 17.2. This entire process takes less than sixty seconds. In this case I took the first list and easily filtered it to include only stocks that had a 30 percent jump in trading volume from the previous day. Now the list is more manageable and will likely give me significantly better opportunities in more active stocks.

ALERTS

I mentioned alerts in Chapter 16. You should also use your computer to give you alerts. Most trading programs provide such a feature. Assume, for example that you are trading four different methods and that you are watching eleven markets

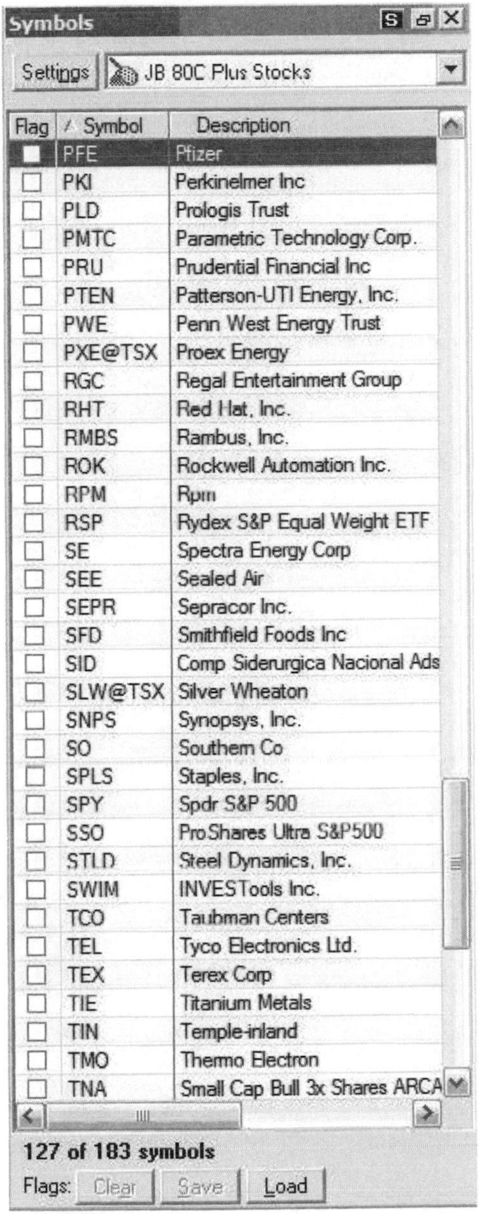

Figure 17.1. Screen of stocks meeting a specific trigger.

Symbols		S 𝖺 X

Settings	JB 80C Plus Stocks	▼

Flag	/ Symbol	Description
☐	AEG	Aegon N.v. Ord
☐	ATI	Allegheny Technologies Click to sor
☐	BGU	Large Cap Bull 3x Shares ARCA
☐	BLK	Blackrock Inc Cl A
☐	BNI	Burlington Northn Santa Fe
☐	CNI	Canadian Natl Railway
☐	CREE	Cree, Inc.
☐	EZPW	EZCORP, Inc.
☐	FNFG	First Niagara Financial Group
☐	GE	General Electric
☐	GWW	Grainger (w.w.)
☐	HSP	Hospira Inc
☐	HSY	Hershey Foods Corp
☐	ISRG	Intuitive Surgical, Inc
☐	IWR	iShares Russell Midcap Index F
☐	IWS	iShares Russell Midcap Value I
☐	IYM	iShares Dow Jones U.S. Basic M
☐	KEY	Keycorp
☐	L	Loews Corporation
☐	MCK	Mckesson Hboc
☐	MT	Mittal Steel Company NV
☐	MVV	ProShares Ultra MidCap400
☐	NWS	News Corporation Limited (The)
☐	NXY	Nexen, Inc.
☐	PFE	Pfizer
☐	RGC	Regal Entertainment Group
☐	ROK	Rockwell Automation Inc.
☐	SEE	Sealed Air
☐	TNA	Small Cap Bull 3x Shares ARCA
☐	WFR	Memc Electronic Materials
☐	WMB	Williams Cos

31 symbols

Figure 17.2. Second stock screen, adding 30 percent trading volume jump as a criterion.

for each of these signals. While this could be done manually it is not readily manageable. Errors are likely. On the other hand, by using an alert feature you could program the computer to track these signals and markets for you. When and if a signal develops based on your criteria the computer will advise you.

PERFORMANCE TRACKING

Like any enterprise, you must track your performance. You cannot know how well your business is going unless you know the bottom line. Here are some specifics to consider on a regular basis. I like to look at these every week, preferably over the weekend:

- How are your specific strategies performing?
- What is their accuracy?
- What are the bottom line profits or losses after commissions and fees?
- Which stocks or commodity sectors are performing best with your methods?
- Are there certain markets that have continued to perform best with certain methods?
- Are your methods robust (i.e., do they recover strongly after a series of losses)?
- How many trades did you make last week?
- How many were profitable? Compared to last week? Last month?
- What was your profit/loss ratio?
- Are your trailing stop strategies working?

- Have you been true to your methods and indicators?

This sounds like a lot of questions to ask, but after a while you'll get used to them, and the reporting tools in most trading platforms will help.

PRIORITY OF METHODOLOGY

Perhaps the most significant conflict that day traders experience is in trying to decide which of the many methods to use. Clearly, the trader who is using only one method does not have this problem. On their other hand, traders who like to track several methods or strategies may be confused when one method says to buy while another says to sell. Similarly once they are in a trade while using one method, another method may give a contrary signal. This can be confusing; I've been there. Here are my suggestions, from experience:

- **Methods can get you in and out**. The day trading methods that got you into a day trade are the methods that should get you out of a market either by the use of an opposite signal in the same method or by a trailing stop or other exit method as part of the same approach.
- **Stick with your method**. Do not use one method to enter a trade and a different method to exit that trade. Different methods consider different aspects of market behavior. Do not mix and match.
- **Using multiple methods is okay**. If you trade using several methods then trade them in different stocks or futures. For example, you can use one method to

trade three or four different markets and you can use an entirely different strategy to trade several entirely different stock or commodities.

- **Don't fiddle too much with bar sizes**. I have not found it productive to compare different time frames within a day in order to confirm trades. In other words, some traders like to look at a thirty-minute chart in order to make a decision in a five- or ten-minute chart. With rare exceptions I have not found this approach to be particularly effective. In fact, it tends to be quite confusing to most traders.

Along with the "pragmatics" discussed in Chapter 16, these concepts will help you run a profitable day trading business.

Chapter **18**

Ten Cardinal Rules of Day Trading

To study day trading theory and method without
practical application is like learning to ride a bicycle
by reading a book. Practice is essential, since it not
only puts you into actual situations that require action
but it also points out your areas of weakness and/or
incomplete understanding.

Many traders believe that "paper trading"—in other words, practice trading—is a necessary step on the road to success. I agree. I hasten to add, however, that paper trading has its limitations as well. The most important of these is the fact that without actual trading, the day trader (or for that matter any type of trader) will not be exposed to the emotional aspect of the business. Only by "being in the trenches" will the trader come face to face with his or her weaknesses.

HOW LONG TO BECOME SUCCESSFUL?

I am often asked how long it will take before a day trader can become successful at this venture. There is no definitive answer to this question. Some day traders can achieve success very quickly, while others may struggle a lifetime without positive results. What is it that separates the winners from the losers? Does success follow on the heels of solid learning and implementing effective strategies? Are there other factors that correlate highly with success as a day trader? Are there unwritten rules or procedures?

Clearly there are many issues that must be considered above and beyond the trading methods and strategies. I have seen traders who use similar trading methods achieve vastly different results. What is it that accounts for these significant differences? How can the playing field be leveled in order to facilitate more consistent and enduring success? Given the nature of the financial markets is it even possible for all traders to win? Or for every winner must there be a loser?

This chapter will address these core issues in an effort to present a realistic view of what it takes to succeed as a day trader. In so doing I will not sugar coat the realities of what we all face when we seek to be successful as day traders.

To a great extent my comments relate to all forms of trading and/or investing. Trading in the day time frame, however, amplifies the issues significantly. How long will it take to become successful as a day trader? The answer depends on complex interaction of numerous variables ranging from the experiential, to the financial, to the pragmatic, to the methods being used. Despite the fact that there is no firm answer to the "how long will it take to succeed" question, I can cite some factors that will lead you in the direction of an answer.

I would like to share with you my list of ten cardinal rules for day traders. Internalizing and implementing these rules will facilitate success and, if you are already successful, they will likely amplify your accomplishments. Note that my rules are not necessarily presented in order of importance.

#1 Do Your Homework

As obvious as this may seem, there are many traders who believe that success will come to them without effort. Day trading must be approached as one approaches any other serious undertaking. If you have a method or methods that are being used in your trading then you must do the necessary work to learn, test, implement, and evaluate these methods. All too often traders will fail to do their homework.

What exactly do I mean by "homework"? It's simple. Homework consists of, among other things, keeping your charts up to date, planning your day, keeping your trading records current, checking your signals as needed, raising stops, etc. Simply stated, you need to be prepared for all your trades for each stage of the cycle—from Set-Up to Trigger to Follow-Through.

If you are not prepared then you will miss moves and/or you will not place stops or trailing stops correctly. The end result will not be to your liking.

While this may seem obvious to you, there are many traders who ignore their homework. I assure you that if you follow their example, you will not succeed as a day trader. If you fail to do your homework, then do not trade!

#2 FOCUS AND SPECIALIZE

You may believe, or be led to believe, that you can day trade in many markets at the same time. While this is indeed possible if you have employees, you can't do it without assistance, particularly when you are just getting started. My suggestion is that you focus on only one or two markets and that you select markets that are not closely correlated with each other. As an example, you might trade one technology stock and one health care stock. In futures you might trade a currency market and the S&P futures. If you choose to trade multiple markets, don't put all your eggs in one basket. In other words, you want to diversify.

#3 BE CONSISTENT

Many would-be day traders are inconsistent in their application of methods. They are also inconsistent in their schedule. Day trading is a business, and it must be approached as a commercial venture. If you want to day trade only one day a week then make it the same day each week. If you want to day trade using one method then use the same method consistently. If you jump from one method and one market to another then you will not be successful other than by sheer luck. If you are consistent then you will give your methods an opportunity to work.

#4 TRADE WITH SUFFICIENT CAPITAL

In terms of importance, this is perhaps the most valuable suggestion I can give you. The sad news about day trading (or for that matter any type of trading) is that aspiring traders begin with insufficient capital. They have been led, either through self-deception or promises by brokers or advisers, to believe that they can make a huge amount of money with minimal starting capital. This is simply not true. You must be prepared to take at least six consecutive losses in your trading. If you are trading a system that has an average loss of $2,000, then an account of $12,000 could be entirely lost.

Furthermore, starting with sufficient capital will give you the leeway you need to avoid making an emotional decision to exit a losing trade prior to what your method suggests as a stop loss or risk amount. Some of the worst mistakes you can make as a day trader are those you make by exiting or entering a trade too soon or too late—resulting in either a smaller profit or a larger loss. If you begin your trading with enough money, you will give yourself enough room to ride a loss and/or a profit until the trade has been completed.

#5 DON'T TRADE ANY STOCK OR FUTURES MARKET THAT SCARES YOU

This may sound somewhat peculiar to you, but nonetheless it is true. The more fear you have, the more inclined you will be to violate your trading rules. Conversely, your likelihood of violating the rules will be less if you have more confidence. If you are frightened by the potential risk in a trade, do not take the trade. As an alternative you can take the trade in a "smaller" security, like a mini futures contract or in an option.

#6 AVOID REACTING TO NEWS REPORTS UNLESS YOU HAVE USED SPECIFIC TRIGGERS

The Internet is a wonderful tool. It allows us to place and execute orders promptly. It allows us to perform market research quickly and efficiently. But the Internet has a dark side. All too often news that can affect the markets reaches traders very rapidly. In turn it causes some markets to swing wildly in one direction or another; sometimes the market wobbles in both directions within a matter of seconds. Such gyrations can affect our indicators temporarily, which in turn may cause traders to take actions that are not in keeping with our methods.

As an example, consider a news item that affects the Swiss franc futures market. You may be trading a system that uses thirty-minute price data. This means that your decisions can only be made at the end of the thirty-minute price period. Bullish news on the Swiss franc comes across the Internet news services, and the Swiss franc futures market begins to move higher. If your computer updates your data tick by tick, then your indicators will also be updated, and you may get a signal to go long. But the signal is not based on the end of the price bar. By the time the thirty minutes has ended, your method may not have triggered. Note that this does not hold true for methods that are designed for entry within a given time frame.

In Chapter 14, I presented one method that relies upon the news. In such cases the news is used as a Set-Up in a specific strategy. You are not reacting to the news without a specific Trigger. Reacting to news is not acceptable unless it is a reaction based on a specific method that has defined entry and exit rules.

#7 AVOID INTERNET CHAT ROOMS

I'll make this rule simple and direct. Most Internet chat rooms dedicated to day trading are visited by traders who are inexperienced, insecure, or insincere. Do you want to be in the company of these individuals? Furthermore, it is a known fact that some traders visit Internet chat rooms in order to spread rumors about a given stock or commodity market in order to support their own position. You must not visit Internet chat rooms. You must not believe anything you hear or see there. You must avoid associating with insecure or novice traders.

#8 A DAY TRADE IS A DAY TRADE

It has been jokingly said that the definition of an investment is "a day trade that ended the day at a loss." It is a sad but true fact that all too often this statement is true. Some day traders believe that a losing trade can be carried overnight if "things look good" or if "it's a good market to own for the longer term" or if "the market is just plain wrong about this one and will get better tomorrow." Collecting losses in this way will not lead to favorable results.

If you enter a position as a day trade, then you must be out by the end of the day. If you carry any trades to the next session, then they must be winning trades. *As a day trader you must not carry losing trades overnight.* It's that simple.

#9 DO NOT COMBINE TIME FRAMES

Some traders would have you believe that in order to be successful you need to combine signals and indicators from one time frame with another. In other words, you may have signals in a ten-minute chart to go long. My experience says that if you have a signal in a ten-minute time frame, you do not need to check any other time frame in order to execute the trade. What happens in one time frame does not necessarily depend on what is happening in another. A large price rally that is taking place in the daily time frame can have a large decline in the ten-minute time frame without necessarily affecting the integrity of the larger time frame.

#10 YOUR BIG MONEY WILL BE MADE IN THE BIG MOVE(S)

You will not be successful as a day trader unless you are able to take advantage of the big moves. The only way that you can get most of them is by riding profitable trades as long as possible, using trailing stops.

It's really very simple. Eighty percent to 90 percent of your profits will be made on 10 percent to 20 percent of your trades. You may find this difficult to accept. You may have been led to believe that you can be successful as a day trader by taking many small profits consistently. That would be true if your losing trades were smaller than your winning trades. The size of your losses will be a function of the stop losses you are using. The reality of today's market is that excessively small stop losses do not work well. They stop you out before the trade is really finished and cut off your chances for the big move.

That said, using excessively large stop losses will lead to larger losses. All too often you will see the profits of many small consecutive winning trades disappear in the form of one large loss. Unless your system is exceptionally accurate (which is unlikely) the majority of your profits will be made on your large winners—make sure your system doesn't take them away from you.

TRADING IN THESE TURBULENT TIMES

Many people have asked me what a severe downturn in the economy and increased market volatility mean for day trading. Although there were numerous warnings prior to the international crisis that surfaced in 2007, investors and traders chose to hide their heads in the sand hoping that somehow things would magically change.

The greatest enemy of the trader is hope. Hope gives us excuses to avoid taking decisive action. It is the underlying culprit that leads to riding losses. Every front has a back. Whereas the front side of the economic crisis threatens the very core of capitalist economic structures, the back side is that it has created unprecedented market volatility. And this volatility, which has expressed itself as the largest intra-day price swings in history, has brought with it the best day trading opportunities I have seen in my lifetime.

It is indeed possible that conditions now extant in the markets may well be the best day trading opportunities we will ever see. Given the time and actions required to rectify the chronic conditions injurious to economic structures, the odds are that intra-day market volatility will continue and that it may, in fact, become even larger. And this all bodes well for the day trader.

That being said, I hasten to add that although crisis creates opportunity, it is only decisive and focused action that turns opportunity into profits. It should not be assumed that the mere presence of massive volatility will lead to profits. Consistent and persistent application of the ingredients necessary for profits from day trading is more important than ever before. Volatility can be your friend if harnessed. It can be your enemy if untamed.

I would like to end this chapter with some practical suggestions, caveats, and advice already presented in different parts of this book. I offer the following to you in the sincere hope that you will take my words seriously and that you will benefit from them. My suggestions are not presented in order of importance. I consider all of them to be important ingredients that will contribute to your success as a day trader.

Organize your trading. Focus on organization. No matter how actively you trade, it is of the utmost importance that you concentrate on the organizational aspects of your trading. What exactly do I mean by organization? It entails the following broad categories, all of which have been discussed in the previous chapters:

- Keeping track of your positions
- Monitoring your positions closely until closed out
- Keeping complete and accurate trading records
- Monitoring your results so that you will know how well (or poorly) your methods are doing
- Keeping a diary of your trades in order to pinpoint any operator errors that may be limiting your profits
- Implementing your plans consistently
- Maintaining an ongoing audit of your trades and positions in order to spot and rectify any errors either on your part or on the part of the broker

Abandon hope; hope is not a strategy. I stated earlier that hope is not an asset to the day trader. I will be even more specific. In order to be successful as a day trader (or for that matter as a trader in any time frame) you must abandon hope. You must never allow yourself to hope that a losing trade will turn into a winning trade. Hope is not part of our Setup, Trigger, Follow-Through equation. As a day trader you must live in reality. There is no reality for the day trader other than profit or loss.

Be an isolationist. As a day trader you may find yourself searching for help or assurance or comfort. Avoid such insecurities. They will not help you. They are desperate expressions of hope and fear. If you isolate yourself from the opinions and expectations of other traders, you will see the truth more clearly and you will avoid being infected by the fear, greed, and hope of other traders.

You may believe that the "experts" who regularly give their opinions on business radio, television, and the Internet know more than you do. You may believe that knowing their thoughts may help you. Don't make that mistake. Their opinions for the intermediate term and long term or even for the short term may not help you at all as a day trader. What happens in the day time frame may not, in most cases, have any significance in the bigger time frame. As a technical trader you must make your decisions based on your indicators and strategies.

In Chapter 14 I discussed a specific day trading method that allows you to use the news to your advantage. Other than this approach I suggest that you avoid other inputs. Some of the best day traders I know trade in isolation. Note that this does not mean that the day trader who listens to the news, who trades based on the news, or who communicates all day with other day traders cannot be successful. It only means that I have not found an objective, operational, and procedural method for doing so. I believe that day trading should be regarded more as science than as art.

Remember that the big money is made in the big move. Unless you have a profit-maximizing strategy, your day trading will be to no avail. You will trade frequently and you will have nothing to show for your efforts. Your broker will make more money than you will. Accept the fact that in the long run, 80 percent to 90 percent of your money will be made on 10 percent to 20 percent of your trades. As a result, you will need the big winners. You will not get the big winners by constantly taking small profits. Implementation of my suggested profit maximizing strategy is a key element to success.

Diversify your trades and methods. I also favor diversification in time frames. You may want to focus on only a limited number of markets and/or methods. However, I strongly suggest that you diversify according to my suggestions as soon as you can. Your goal as a day trader, above and beyond profits, should be consistency.

Don't fall victim to the "small stop loss" illusion. Some traders would have you believe that a small stop loss will be your key to success. In today's volatile markets, small stop losses do not protect you, they hurt you. How large should your stop losses be? The stop loss must be a function of your system or method. Your stop loss must never be based only on what you can afford to risk. This is one of the most important things I can tell you. For example, if your system requires you to use a $500 stop loss on a trade, then either use that stop loss or do not take the trade. Do not arbitrarily say that you will risk $250 rather than $500 because you cannot afford the $500. Such behavior will lead to failure.

Don't assume that day trading is the best thing for you. Too many traders believe that day trading is the only vehicle that will lead to success. Clearly this is not the case. Day trading is not right for all traders. Some traders simply do not possess or cannot develop the emotional and behavioral fortitude that are necessary for success as a day trader.

Remember that how you exit day trades is critically important. I illustrated and discussed a number of viable day trading methods in this book. I have also emphasized the importance of using a variety of exit strategies as a means of maximizing profits. How you exit your day trades is of the utmost importance. You will need to consistently maximize profits by using a variety of exit techniques.

Remember and apply the "danger zone" concept. I believe that my "danger zone" concept is one of the keys to day-trading success. The more often you can get out of the danger zone and ride the free trade, the more often you put yourself in a position of capturing the big trades. Even though you may be repeatedly stopped out at break even, you will, sooner or later, catch the big moves that are so essential to success as a day trader.

Do not assume that more is better. While there are day traders who have achieved considerable success trading as much as possible and trading as many shares or contracts as they can, this is not the only approach to success, and it may not necessarily be the best approach. Unless your methods are consistently accurate and unless you are able to trade large positions while consistently limiting losses, you will not be successful simply because you are taking frequently and trading large positions. I believe that you will be better off focusing on quality as opposed to quantity.

Abandon the "Holy Grail" approach to selecting a method. You may be tempted to search for the ultimate or perfect day trading method. It does not exist. You may be seduced by those who claim that they have new and amazing day trading methods. The odds are that they are wrong and are trying to take advantage of you. If, however, you find yourself believing the claims then investigate before you invest. Look at the trading style of the program and see if it fits with your financial abilities. Look at the risks and the consistency of the methods. Ask the seller of the system or method or seminar or course to show you some signals as they occur. Ask if all the trading rules are objective. Only in so doing can you realistically evaluate the method or system.

Understand the meaning of discipline and the origin of confidence. In my view, lack of discipline is a symptom. The underlying cause of poor discipline is lack of confidence. Confidence grows from competence. Competence grows from solid and objective methods that are a function of effective and profitable methodologies. Unless you have an objective and effective arsenal of trading methods and procedures you will not have the confidence from which profits will flow. If you have the confidence then you will have the discipline to implement your methods with discipline. In short, discipline can only come from confidence and confidence can only come from objective and effective trading methods.

While there are many other suggestions I could give you based on my forty years in the markets, I believe that those given above are the most important.

As market technology and software technology continue to develop at a fast pace, numerous advances will be made in all aspects of the trading arena. Where such advances can benefit your trading, I encourage you to use them to your advantage. As in all cases, however, take time to evaluate such advances in terms of whether they are real benefits as opposed to hollow promises.

Conclusion

The world of day trading is indeed a challenging one. Day traders are continuously bombarded by news, fundamental market data, rumors, and trading programs that create numerous opportunities. Yet, these opportunities are fraught with risk. Given the lightning speed of news delivery via Internet as well as the ability to execute trading orders instantly, day trading opportunities are more plentiful than ever.

Clearly the risks as well as the opportunities demand knowledge, structure, discipline, and profitable methodologies. Key trading tools for success and a clear and effective risk management and profit maximizing strategy form the essential underpinnings of a profitable day trading program. Although I believe that the information, methods, and systems I have provided in this book will get you started on the road to success, this is just the first step. The systems and methods must be put into practice with consistency, organization, and persistence. In short, there is no substitute for practice!

There are five key areas to success as a day trader. This book has attempted to cover each in as much detail as possible. By way of review here are those areas along with a brief commentary on their importance:

1. Methodology: I have provided you with a number of day-trading methods. My goal in so doing has been to give you a step-by-step procedure by which day trades can be implemented, executed, and managed from the standpoint of risk and reward. I have attempted to be as objective as possible. Take to heart my suggestion that unless a trading method is 100 percent objective in its rules and implementation, your odds of success will be limited. The less objective your methods are, the less likely you will be to succeed. Success in day trading (in fact in all types of trading) is limited by the emotional responses that are born from subjective decisions.

2. Structure: The essential underpinning of all day trades is a solid structure within which the decision making process operates. To this end I have given you the Setup, Trigger, and Follow-Through model. Using this model will not only give you 100 percent objectivity but it will also allow you to learn from your mistakes through the procedural clarity it provides. Without a trading model the odds are that you will lose money whether you are a day trader or a position trader.

3. Focus: Most day traders believe that more is better when it comes to trading. They feel that they must try to take advantage of every price swing and/or every opportunity that comes their way. In attempting to actualize this feeling they tend to become scattered in their attention and frequently either miss changes in their indicators or their error rate increases. I believe that in day trading, "less is more." By this I mean that you are much better off focusing on a few markets rather than many and on a few opportunities rather than many. Given that most day-trading

methods are labor and attention intensive, you will need focus as opposed to a diffuse "broad brushstroke" approach.

4. Time frame: The time frame in which you operate as a day trader is also critically important. As noted above, as a day trader you will be presented with numerous opportunities in numerous time frames. You will need to decide whether you want to trade in the five-minute, ten-minute, thirty-minute, sixty-minute, or other time frames. Different time frames will give different signals. What may be a buying opportunity in the thirty-minute time frame may be a selling opportunity in the ten-minute time frame. The more time frames you use in your work the more confused you will become. The time frame that gets you into a day trade should be the time frame that gets you out of a day trade. Mixing time frames does not, in my humble opinion, lead to clarity; rather it is the first step on the road to confusion. Confusion will lead to losses.

5. Profit-maximizing strategy: It is utterly essential that you have and use a profit maximizing strategy for all of your day trades. Eighty percent to 90 percent of your money as a day trader will be made on 10 percent to 20 percent of your trades. Without the large winning trades, your success as a day trader will be limited. You will generate many small profits, which will be balanced off by the cost of commissions and small losses. Unless you have a clear and concise method for maximizing profits, your efforts as a day trader will not be rewarded.

PRACTICAL CONSIDERATIONS

Above and beyond the critical issues I have noted above, there are several other practical but nonetheless significant issues. I've dealt with these in previous chapters, but they are of sufficient importance that they bear repeating:

Consistency in day of week. Some day traders believe that they can day trade when they have the time to do so. I believe otherwise. Day trading is a job. It must be approached as such. If you believe that you can day trade when you feel like doing so then I suggest you are not approaching this venture from a standpoint of a business enterprise but as a hobby. Why do I say this? We don't know all of the patterns that exist in the markets. There may be underlying day of week patterns. Not knowing whether or not these patterns exist, you must make the commitment to trade every day or, if you cannot do that, do not undertake day trading.

Consistency in method. Day traders (in fact all traders) have a tendency to jump from one system or method to another, often in response to a series of losses. When the temptation to do so is greatest, the odds are also greatest that you should not do so. Consistency in trading method is of paramount importance. Remember that even the best trading methods can be incorrect up to seven times in a row. Be prepared.

Sufficient trading capital. Some trading advisers and/or brokers may attempt to convince you that you can begin your day trading venture on a shoestring budget. This is not true. The less money you fund your account with the lower will be your odds of success.

Brokerage account. Naturally, if you plan to day trade you will need to have an account. Take time to make certain that you explore your account options carefully. There are many choices, many different commission cost possibilities, and numerous platforms you can use for order entry. Some broker will provide you with price quotes and the ability to do research on trades and systems. Generally their fees will be higher. Consider your choices carefully. Evaluate all the options; sometimes cheaper is not better, but more expensive is not always best.

Limitations on day trading. There are rules that limit "pattern day trading" as a function of your account size. Be certain you are aware of these rules. In addition, some brokerage houses place restrictions of their own on day trading as well as on short selling. Be informed to avoid nasty surprises.

Trading software. There are many choices of trading and charting software that are available to the day trader. Some have features you do not need. There is no need to pay for what you will not use. You may believe that you can begin your day trading venture by using free charting software that's available on the Internet. In most cases the price data for these programs is delayed by as much as thirty minutes. If your data is delayed then you are not getting the timely information you need for success. Investigate all of the relevant issues before you buy or subscribe to a charting package. I have given you a few suggestions in my Resources list. Always sign up for a trial period before you commit to buying any software package.

Trading systems. Many vendors offer systems that will give you their buy and sell signals. These are usually quite expensive. Many are optimized to show the best performance and they will not go forward in real time with results as back tested historically. Be careful of these programs. They rarely work. Remember that you want to learn how to fish on your own rather than have a software program trade for you. Very often these programs are "black box." This means that they generate buy and sell signals for you but you have no idea why. Is that what you want?

Speed of data transmission. The bottom line for most day traders is speed of execution. If you are slow to respond to an opportunity then you may not get the best price executions. Poor price executions add up to lost profits or increased losses. A data line that does not give you quick or up-to-date price quotes will be a detriment to your performance. A brokerage account that cannot fill your orders almost instantly will be costly to you. Speed of data delivery and speed of order execution are critically important to your success. In this case the rule is "the faster the better."

ARE YOU A DAY TRADER?

Finally, I must address an issue that will, sooner or later, confront all day traders. That issue is whether to take your loss or to hold your losing trade(s).

Taking a day trade loss will always be a negative experience. It cannot be avoided. Either you are a day trader or you are not a day trader. One of the largest losses I have ever taken was a day trade that showed a $500 loss at the end of the day. I failed to take the loss at the end of the day since I could not admit to failure. I looked for and found numerous excuses to keep the trade. The loss grew larger and it was eventually closed out as a $5,000 loss. Shame on me. That was a mistake I never made again. Learn from my mistake.

Glossary

While I have not used all these terms in this book, I have included them in the glossary as a general reference, should you come across them in other day trading literature and wonder what they mean.

Analyst. An individual who utilizes fundamental and/or technical analysis to forecast stock or commodity prices, trends, company earnings, chart patterns, timing signals, etc.

Ask. The price at which an individual, group, or firm is willing to sell a financial instrument (i.e., stock, commodity, option, FOREX contract).

Auction market. A physical market, such as the NYSE and the AMEX or other futures or stock exchanges, where a specialist or market maker acts as an auctioneer, coordinating buying and selling to those making bids and offers for the purchase and/or sale of financial instruments.

Bear market. A declining market or, more technically, a market that has declined 20 percent from its previous peak price.

Bid/offer. A bid is an offer to buy at a given price, whereas an offer is an order to sell at a given price. Buyers bid for a given financial instrument, while sellers offer a given financial instrument.

Breakout. When the price of a financial instrument moves past a previous support or resistance level or high or low price.

Broker. A salesperson who deals in securities or commodities.

Bull market. A market in which prices are generally rising.

Buy and hold. A strategy involving the purchase of financial instruments for the long term, typically for years at a time. Buy and hold can also occur on an intra-day basis as long as positions are liquidated by the close of the session.

Correction. A decline in an up trending market or a rally in a down trending market.

Covering a short. When short sellers repurchase a financial instrument to replace or cover the market that was sold short. This is another way of stating that a short position is being exited.

Curve fitting. (Also called optimizing.) The act of fitting a trading system to past data. When a trading system developer optimizes a system, he or she does so in order to generate a set of system rules that have performed well on historical data. Although the system appears to have worked well in the past, it is in fact fitted to historical data, which means that the system may not perform well in the future. To a given extent, most system testing involves some degree of optimization and curve fitting.

Day trade. A trade that is entered and exited on the same day. It does not mean that the trade will always be entered on the opening and exited on the close, or that it will not entail risk. Twenty-four-hour trading has blurred the definition of the term. By definition, a trade is no longer a day trade if carried through to the next trading session. Day trades may be entered at any time during the day, but they must be closed out by the end of the day.

Day trader. A trader who day trades.

Day trading. The act of entering and exiting positions on the same day.

Downtick. When the sale price of a market is lower than the last sale price.

Equity. The amount of money in a trading or investing account.

Equity position. Stock ownership of part of a company by means of holding the stock of that company.

Fundamental analysis. An analysis process that looks at the fundamentals or basic issues of a company or market such as price-to-earnings (P/E) ratio, future earnings potential, dividends, income, debt management, market share for stocks. For futures such factors as weather, exports, imports, government policies, supply and demand, and crop conditions are used in the process. Fundamental analysis attempts to determine where the price of a market should be, based on the current characteristics and future potential.

Fundamentalist. Someone who looks at a market's fundamentals to determine where the price should be or where it is likely to be in the future.

Gap. When the opening price of a market is higher than the previous day's high or lower than the previous day's low.

Intermediate-term trading. An intermediate-term trade is one usually held for several months. Many traders, money managers, and investors prefer such trades. Intermediate-term traders seek to take advantage of larger price swings but do not wish to hold positions for several years or more. They seek to maximize their capital by holding trades for larger moves over a period of months, thereby attempting to capitalize on larger market swings.

Investing. A stock market investor can hold positions for several years or even for many decades. What the day trader does is the antithesis of what the investor does, but with one exception. They both try to make money but they approach the task in distinctly different ways and with markedly different methods. Generally speaking, commodity traders are not considered investors. Day traders are not considered investors.

IPO. An IPO is an initial public offering of a stock, or the first time that the general public can purchase shares in a company when it becomes publicly traded.

Keltner. Chester Keltner, a market analyst whose work was developed in the 1950s and which has become widely followed since the 1980s.

Limit order. The buyer or seller of a financial instrument sets a maximum price at which he or she is willing to buy, or the minimum price at which he is willing to sell.

Liquid. A market that has sufficient trading activity (volume) to allow for relatively easy entry and exit.

Long-term trading. A long-term trader may hold positions for several years, rolling contracts forward as they approach expiration. What the day trader does is the antithesis of what the long-term trader does.

MACD. Moving average convergence divergence; a market timing indicator.

Market entry. Market entry means simply to establish a new long or short position. There are many different types of orders that may be used for entering and exiting markets.

Market exit. Market exit means to close out an existing long or short position. Again, there are many different types of orders that may be used for entering and exiting markets.

Market order. An order to trade a financial instrument at whichever price happens to be prevailing at the time the order is received.

Market timing. A strategy that attempts to buy stocks at the bottom of a bear market and sell them at the top of a bull market. This strategy assumes that tops and bottoms can be easily picked.

Momentum. A combination of volume and volatility in a market that keeps its price continuing in the same direction.

Momentum indicator. A mathematical method of quantifying momentum.

Glossary

Moving averages (MA). Moving averages have many and varied applications in trading. There are numerous applications for buying and selling on penetrations of MA applications.

Offer. A price at which someone is willing to buy stock.

Optimization. (See curve fitting.)

Oscillate. To oscillate is to move back and forth between extremes.

Overbought. After a market has been moving higher, prices eventually go "too high" to be sustained, and the market is said to be overbought, which suggests that a drop could follow. This is a relative term that rarely has a purely objective definition.

Oversold. After a market has been moving lower, prices eventually reach a point at which traders believe prices are too low to be sustained. The stock is said to be oversold, which could mean that a rise could follow. This is a relative term that rarely has a purely objective definition.

Over-trading. Trading simply for the sake of trading and thereby trading too often.

Position. Holding shares or contracts in a given market or markets.

Position trader. As soon as a day trader holds a position overnight, he or she becomes a position trader. A position trader

331

holds trades for an extended period ranging from several weeks to as much as several years. The position trader can also be called an investor in stocks.

Position trading. When day trades are held overnight, they become position trades; therefore, when a trader holds his or her trades longer than a day (i.e., usually several weeks to years) it is called position trading.

Profit taking. When a recent run-up in a market brings sellers onto the market to take profits before the price moves back down.

Quote. The current price, bid, and offer on a market.

Rally. A run-up in the price of a market.

Resistance. The price level at which a market is expected to halt its upward trend and from which prices are expected to move lower at best or sideways at worst.

Reversal. When the price of a market reaches a given level and turns around from there.

Scalping. Ultra-short-term trading for very small but intra-day profits.

SEC. Securities and Exchange Commission.

Securities. Stocks or equities.

Sell-off. A rapid decline in prices.

Short. To sell a market that you do not own in the hope of repurchasing it at a lower price and profiting from the difference.

Short-term trader. One who trades for relatively short-term market swings of two to ten days' duration. There is no firm definition of the exact length of time short-term traders hold their positions.

Short-term trading. Short-term trading, as opposed to day trading or position trading, is trading for relatively short-term market swings of two to ten days' duration. Again, there is no firm definition of the exact length of time for short-term trading. The distinction between short-term trading and position trading is not as precise as is the distinction between day trading and all other types of trading.

Slippage. The tendency of a market to fall or rise very quickly, picking buy and sell stop orders very quickly. Hence, a $100 deduction for slippage means deducting $100 from every trade in a hypothetical back-test in order to represent more accurately what might have happened. A market that tends to have too much slippage is, therefore, a market in which quick and sudden price moves tend to result in price fills that are unexpectedly or unreasonably far away from your price orders.

Spread. The difference between the bid and the ask price.

Stochastics. The stochastic indicator (SI) is basically a price-derived oscillator expressed in percentages. SI values approach 0 and 100 as limits. The SI consists of two values, %K and %D. The SI period can be adjusted as desired. The shorter the period, the more the SI will fluctuate. If one or both SI lines have been above 75 percent and one or both cross below 75 percent on a closing basis for the given period, then sells can be considered. If one or both SI lines have been below 25 percent and if one or both cross above 25 percent on a closing basis, then buys can be considered. Note that a more conservative variation of this application would be to require both SI lines to cross as opposed to requiring just one line to cross. If price makes a new high for a given time period but SI does not, then a top may be forming. If price makes a new low for a given period of time and SI does not, then a bottom may be forming.

Stock split. When a stock's price reaches a level that appears expensive to the general public, a company often divides the price but increases the number of shares.

Stop order. A sell order typically placed just below where a current price is, to enable the seller to exit the market if a price decline begins, or above the current price if one is in a short position.

Support. The price level at which a market is expected to halt its declining trend and from which prices are expected to move higher at best or sideways at worst.

Technical analysis. Utilizes charts and graphs to determine where a particular market's price is likely to be headed in the future.

Technician. An individual who uses technical analysis to predict market trends.

Timing indicators or timing signals. A timing indicator is defined as any specific technique, whether fundamental or technical, which objectively indicates market entry, exit, or the underlying condition (i.e., bullish, bearish, neutral) of a given stock, futures, options or index. A timing indicator can also be called a timing signal, as the terms are used interchangeably.

Trading range. This term is used to describe primarily lateral movement in a market's price, with limited up and down movements.

Trading systems. A trading system is an organized methodology containing specific market entry and exit indicators, as well as an operational set of procedures (called rules), including, but not limited to, various risk management methods (follow-up stop-loss), and procedures. A trading system is implemented by following specific timing signals that dictate market entry and exit. Trading systems must be necessarily rigid in their construction for the purpose of delineating specific procedures which, theoretically, should lead to profitable trading, provided the system is functioning as intended or tested. A trading system must be systematic or it is not a trading system, regardless of what the individual who professes to be trading a "system" may think.

Trading technique. A trading technique is a fairly loose collection of procedures that assists traders in making decisions about market entry or exit. Frequently, a trading technique consists of one or more timing indicators combined with general entry and exit rules and/or risk management procedures. A trading technique is, therefore, not a trading system, but rather an approach to trading that is generally objective but not nearly as precise or rigid as is a trading system.

Trendline. A line drawn across either the price peaks of a market trend or the price bottoms, to emphasize the overall trend.

Upbid. When the bid price is higher than the previous bid price.

Uptick. When the sales price is continuing to rise after a previous rise.

Volatility. The price range at which variations in a market's price occur. The larger the range, the higher the volatility.

Resources

READING SUGGESTIONS

Bernstein, Jacob, *The Compleat Day Trader*. McGraw-Hill, 1995.

Bernstein, Jacob, *The Compleat Day Trader II*. McGraw-Hill, 1998.

Bernstein, Jacob, *The Compleat Guide to Day Trading Stocks*. McGraw-Hill, 2001.

Bernstein, Jacob, *Profit in the Futures Markets!* Bloomberg Press, 2002.

Bernstein, Jacob, *Momentum Stock Selection*. McGraw-Hill 2002.

Williams, Larry, *Long-Term Secrets to Short-Term Trading*. John Wiley & Sons, Inc., 1999.

RECOMMENDED WEBSITES

www.jakebernstein.com

www.seasonaltrader.com

www.genesisft.com

www.equis.com

JAKE BERNSTEIN RECOMMENDED TRADING WEBINARS

Profit Maximizing Strategies Webinar

Four Best Timing Triggers Webinar

Short-term Day Trading Webinar

Information available at *www.jakebernstein.com.*

Index

%D line (signal line, slow stochastic indicator), 207, 209–11

%K line (main line, fast stochastic oscillator), 207, 209–11, 214, 216

%K-%D crossover method, 211–14

200 period moving average, 114–16

75/25 method, 209–11

8 open/close indicator, 268–73

80/20 method, 209–11

A,B,C,D charting method, 180–84, 199

Active markets, 54, 137, 201

Alerts, 287, 296–299

Back testing, 34, 36, 62–64

Bearish divergence, 155, 164, 167, 168, 169, 170, 171, 172, 173, 177–78, 179, 192, 202
   choosing sell point after, 184, 185
   price and, 156

A Beginner's Guide to Day Trading Online (Turner), 9

Break-even target, 263, 264, 266

Bullish divergence, 154, 161–66, 171, 172, 173, 177–84, 188, 190, 191
   choosing buy point after, 180–84
   finding periods of, 182–83
   price and, 156

Business model, 293

Business processes implementation, 294

Buy point/signal/trigger, 89–90, 120, 174, 178–84, 188, 189, 191, 232, 236
   choosing after bullish divergence, 180–84
   identifying, 178–80
   stochastic indicator and, 209–11, 212, 217, 218, 219, 220

Buy set-up, 88

Buy stop, 127

Capital, trading with sufficient, 307, 321–22

Chat rooms, avoiding, 311

Commissions, fees, and costs, 20, 48–49, 50–51, 286, 293, 322

Commodities markets, 54, 55

Competition, 24

The Compleat Day Trader
(Bernstein), 10
Computers and software, 68,
284–90, 295–299, 322–23
Confidence, 38, 40, 316–17
Confusion, 6–7, 199
Consistency, 28, 34, 56, 203, 306,
321
Corn futures, 57
Crude oil futures, 57

Daily price reversal pattern, 69
Danger zone concept, 194, 195–
96, 266, 278–79, 315
Day of Week Pattern (DOW),
123, 125–37, 321
defined, 126
examples, 130–34
implementation of, 136–37
pros and cons of, 127–28
Discipline, 37–38, 40, 42–43, 50,
186–87, 199, 316–17
Divergence, 151–75, 177–92,
193–204. *See also* Bearish
divergence; Bullish divergence;
Momentum divergence timing
method; Moving average
convergence divergence
applying, 170–74
examples of trading with,
197–201
pointers for trading with,
201–4

review of, 186–87
short-term with STF, 60–61
Diversification, 276–78, 314
Don't Sell Stocks on Monday
(Hirsch), 125
Dutch Tulip Mania, 2–3

Electronic trading account
platforms, 285
E-Mini NASDAQ futures, 57
E-Mini Russell futures, 57
E-Mini S&P 500 futures, 55, 57,
59, 93, 96, 144, 145, 188, 189,
209, 210, 215, 268, 269, 270,
271, 272
Emotional responses, 86, 140–
44, 146, 319
Entry strategies, 61, 64, 78, 194
Exit strategies, 61, 64, 78, 81–82,
194, 199, 216, 259–73
for gap trading, 91–92,
100–105
for single unit trading, 263–64
stochastic POP and, 216, 218,
219, 220
for three-unit trading, 265–67
trend breakout method and,
236–39
for two-unit trading, 264

Fear, 307
Filters, computer, 287, 288,
295–96

First profitable opening (FPO)
  strategy, 91–92, 199
Focus, 306, 319–20
Follow-Through (F), 81–82, 120,
  260
  Day of Week Pattern and, 127
  described, 78–79
  divergence and, 193–204
  for gap trading, 90, 100–105
Foreign currency (FOREX)
  market, 2, 18–19, 54, 57, 58, 68
Free trade, 195–96
Futures markets, 19, 57–58, 100,
  307

Gap days, 89, 107
Gap day trading, 59–60, 85–107
  characteristics of, 107
  examples, 93–100
  size of gap, 92–93
  track records, 105–7
  types of gaps, 87–88
Gap-down openings, 86, 87, 89
Gap-up openings, 86, 87, 88, 89
Gold futures, 57

Half-position closeout, 264
Highlight bars, 289, 290
Hirsch, Yale, 125
Holy Grail approach, 316

Impulse trades, avoiding, 44–45,
  50

Information sources, 284–86
Insider information, 246–47
Internet, 5–6, 26, 284, 308, 309
The Investor's Quotient
  (Bernstein), 42

Keltner, Chester (Keltner
  method), 226–29

Lane, George, 205, 206, 211, 214
Leading indicators, 173, 174–75
Lies, debunking, 70–72
Liquidity, lack of, 54
Losses, carrying, 309, 324

Margins, 20
Markets, 53–61
  applying methods to, 59–61
  best futures, 57–58
  characteristics of best, 54–57
  choice of, 261
  myths of, 69–70
Market volatility, 20, 35, 36,
  55–56, 311
Markovitz, Harry, 276
Momentum (MOM), 77, 118,
  120, 122, 152, 156–58, 161. See
  also Price and momentum
Momentum Breakout Point
  (MBP), 184
Momentum divergence timing
  method, 156, 177–92
  buy point and, 178–84

sell point and, 184
Momentum indicator, 75, 79, 118, 152–56, 161, 204
Moving average (MA), 70, 77, 113–16, 267–68, 269
Moving average channel (MAC) method, 60, 116–23
Moving average convergence divergence (MACD), 151, 152–53, 156, 158–61, 204, 223
Myths
day trading, 66–68
market, 69–70
small stop loss advantage, 35–37

NASDAQ futures, 57
News, 20, 67–68, 86, 174, 245–58
avoiding reactions without triggers, 308
common reactions to, 247–48
examples of reactions to, 250–58
isolation from, 44–45, 313–14
market trends and bias, 248

Objectivity, 64–66, 194, 319
Optimization, 62, 63
Order types, 288
Organization, 41–42, 50, 292, 293–94, 312
Overbought (OB) fallacy, 206, 208–9, 211, 214

Overseas markets, 57–58
Oversold (OS) fallacy, 206, 208–9, 211, 214
Over-trading, 49–50, 51

Paper trades, 63–64, 304
Parabolic trailing stop, 268, 270
Pareto Principle, 262
Performance tracking, 299–300
Planning, 46
Position size, 261–62, 278–79
Position trading, 136, 266–67
Price and momentum, 75, 79, 152–56, 174–75
declining together, 158–61
divergence in, 161–66
Profit-maximizing strategies, 61, 64, 78–79, 123, 136, 314, 320
limitations on, 260–61
with money management programs, 279–83
Profit taking, 263, 264, 265–66
Profit targets, 262, 263–64, 265, 266

Record-keeping, 294–95
Risk, 2–3, 13, 57, 58, 78, 279
Rules for day trading, 305–10

Scans, computer, 295–96
Screeners, 288–90

Sector leadership, primary
market in, 56
Sell point/signal/trigger, 90,
118, 120, 174, 179, 192, 202,
232, 236
choosing after bearish
divergence, 184, 185
stochastic indicator and, 209–
11, 212, 217, 218, 219, 220
Sell set-up, 88
Sell stop, 127
Set-Up (S)
Day of Week Pattern and, 127
described, 75–77
with divergence, 151–75
gap, 88–89
Setup, Trigger, and Follow-
Through (STF) method, 40,
46, 63, 64, 65, 73–82, 232, 293,
319
for Day of Week Pattern,
126–27
description of elements,
75–79
example of, 79–80
faulty trading corrected by,
80–81
in intermediate and long-term
trading, 81
short-term divergence with,
60–61
Short sales, 87, 250, 251
Soybean futures, 57, 234, 237

Specialization, 306
S&P 500 futures, 31, 33, 55, 57,
59, 68, 79–80, 117, 118, 121,
126, 230, 231, 235, 239
Spread, 25, 109
Stochastic indicator (SI), 204,
205–20
definition and characteristics,
206–8
traditional approaches to,
209–14
Stochastic POP Method (SP),
206, 209, 214–20
Stocks/stock market, 19, 54, 55,
58, 307
Stop losses, 90, 101, 262, 264–65
examples of differing
amounts, 29–33
excessively large, 310
small, 35–37, 67, 310, 314–15
Stress, 24, 46–47, 50
Structure, 73, 74, 293–94, 319
Subjective judgments, 260, 319
Support-and-resistance trading,
109, 110–13, 114, 122, 223,
224, 225, 227
Swing trading, 60, 223, 226

Technical analysis, 61–62
Thirty-minute breakout for S&P
500 futures, 59
Three-unit trading, 265–67, 278
Time frames, 196–97, 279, 301,

309–10, 320

Timing indicators, 65

Trade size, 196–97

Trade the news–fade the news
method, 248–50, 251

Trading methods, 319, 321
applying to markets, 59
defined, 65
diversification across, 277,
314
priority of, 300–1

Trading ranges, 54–55, 203

Trading systems, 43, 50, 65

Trailing stops, 80, 186, 199, 216,
229, 262, 263–64, 266, 286,
310
defined, 267
strategies for, 267–73

Treasury bonds, 30-year, 57, 115,
202, 217, 240

Treasury notes, 10-year, 57, 150

Trend breakout method, 222–42
definition and characteristics
of, 222–26
filtering, 237–39

Trend line, 110–13

Trigger (T), 308
Day of Week Pattern and, 127
described, 77
gap, 89–90
Momentum (*see* Momentum
divergence timing method)
volume spikes and, 146–48

"Turn Around Tuesday," 69

Turner, Toni, 9

Volume, 56, 201, 203

Volume spikes, 139–50
operational definition of,
144–46
testing, 148
using, 146–48

Weakest link in the chain
principle, 37–38, 40, 41, 157

Wilder, J. Welles, 268

Williams, Larry, 87

Williams Accumulation/
Distribution (AD), 118

About the Author

Jacob Bernstein is president of MBH Commodity Advisors Inc. and Bernstein Investments Inc. Born in Europe in 1946, Bernstein moved to Canada and then to the United States. He has authored more than thirty-five books on trading, investing, investor psychology and economic forecasts, including the classic *The Compleat Day Trader*. His books have been published by Wiley and Sons, McGraw-Hill, Simon and Schuster, Dow-Irwin, New York Institute of Finance, Entrepreneur Press, and Harper-Collins.

His newsletters and advisory services are read internationally by traders, investors, brokers, financial institutions, and money managers. Bernstein's consulting clients include some of the largest hedge funds, brokerage firms, market analysts, banks, and professional traders in the world.

He maintains a web presence at Jake Bernstein on Futures (*www.trade-futures.com*) and his stock market advisory 2Chimps".com (*www.2chimps.com*), Seasonaltrader.com, and Patterns4Profit.com.

Bernstein has been a featured and/or a keynote speaker at leading investment conferences and trading seminars the world over. He has held more than 500 of his own seminars since the 1970s, and is considered a leading educator, market analyst and researcher in the field of stocks and futures.

His clients include some of the world's largest banks and brokerage firms as well as professional traders, major hedge funds, and money managers. He has developed and popularized a number of innovative market indicators and concepts.

He has authored articles in *Futures Magazine, Money Maker, Stocks and Commodities, Barron's Financial Weekly, FarmFutures,* and other leading financial publications. He is a guest commentator on business radio, Internet radio, podcasts, and television. He has appeared on numerous radio and television business shows, including Financial News Network, Jag. FN, Web.fn, CNBC, CNN (London), WBBM Radio Chicago and Wall Street Week, as well as numerous radio and television shows. He has been a keynote speaker, workshop leader, or organizer of numerous investment and trading conferences throughout the world. Bernstein's seminars and speaking engagements in 2005–2007 have been held in Singapore, Milan, London, Rotterdam, Chicago, Los Angeles, Dallas, Orlando, Ft. Lauderdale, Denver, New York, and Houston.

Bernstein holds a BA degree in clinical and experimental psychology from the University of Illinois with work toward a MA degree in the same field.